EXECUTIVE TEMPING

A Guide for Professionals

Saralee Terry Woods

JOHN WILEY & SONS, INC.

New York • Chichester • Weinheim • Brisbane • Singapore • Toronto

This book is printed on acid-free paper. ∞

Published by John Wiley & Sons, Inc.

Published simultaneously in Canada.

This publication is designed to provide accurate and authoritative information in regard to the subject matter covered. It is sold with the understanding that the publisher is not engaged in rendering legal, accounting, or other professional services. If legal advice or other expert assistance is required, the services of a competent professional person should be sought.

Library of Congress Cataloging-in-Publication Data:

Woods, Saralee T., 1955–
    Executive temping : a guide for professionals / Saralee T. Woods.
      p. cm.
    Includes bibliographical references and index.
    ISBN 0-471-24157-1 (pbk. : alk. paper)
    1. Temporary employment. 2. Professional employees.
  HD5854.W66   1998
  650.14—dc21   97-50521

Printed in the United States of America.

10 9 8 7 6 5 4 3 2 1

For my family:

Larry, Rachel, Allen, Sarah,
Caesar, and Cleo

Preface

THE ECONOMY OF THE UNITED STATES FROM 1992 TO 1997 HAS been the best in the history of the nation. Concurrently with these unparalleled "good times," American businesses have been redefining their relationships with employees on every level. Temp agencies, now called staffing services, have become an integral part of the marketplace from Main Street to Wall Street. For most companies the issue is not whether to use temps, but rather how many, in which areas, and for what terms. The employment structure of business has been forever redefined.

My entry into the business of temp services started 10 years ago. I had worked in a political campaign where my candidate lost and immediate unemployment commenced. I found myself "between jobs"—the euphemism for being out of work. With a master's degree in planning and no immediate prospects, I did not consider the world of temping, because I incorrectly thought that temping was only for secretaries.

I was fortunate to enter the business of employment agencies, as the staffing industry was called then, and I found a world of opportunities. In 1995, a group of professional technical people asked me to speak on the subject of temporary employment. It was astounding how little information was available in print regarding temporary employment. A search for an industry book on temporary services was fruitless. I saw a compelling need for the ideas in this book.

Executive Temping as a title embodies the concept of this new business segment of the 1990s and the importance of the professional technical temporary employee in the financial structure. The book addresses the paradigmatic shift in American and worldwide employment structure. Temping reached adulthood in the 1990s and will be a dominant employment segment in the 21st century.

Acknowledgments

S O MANY PEOPLE HELPED ME WITH THIS BOOK. A SPECIAL THANK you to my editor, Mike Hamilton, and my fantastic literary agent, Pema Browne. I owe so many people who have been my teachers in the staffing industry: Jane Jones, Ted Jones, Gayle Hall, Bernice Howard, Bill Wood, Sandra Brown, Joanne Pridgen, Lynda Thornhill, Sue Goodrich Ward, Ramona Harris, Janie Craighead, Darlene Hendricks, Debbie Worley, and Alecia Teal.

The people in the staffing industry who were interviewed for this book were most helpful. They are Carl Camden, Executive Vice President of Sales and Marketing for Kelly Services; Marty Rome, Director of Public Relations for Kelly Services, Inc.; Joe Freedman, president of Amicus Legal Staffing, Inc.; Greta Kreske, manager of strategic information for Manpower International; Paul Sharps, president of Global Dynamics; Fred Sussman, president of Information Technology; Jack Maxwell, president of Maxwell Medical Staffing; Bill Wood, President of Wood Personnel; Mark Nightingale, area manager of Robert Half Accountemps; Jane Jones with Creative Training Solutions; as well as those who helped from Olsten, AccuStaff, Norrell, and Adecco.

I also want to thank Tony Lee, editor of *National Business Employment Weekly*, for his patience and many interviews as we discussed various trends about employment. Jerry L. Thomas, chief operating officer/senior consultant from The Strickland Group, taught me how his business is to manage change. My friends Debbie Runions and Martha Deacon used their own writing skills to critique and offer suggestions. Frank Woods helped in many areas, from titles to marketing. John Hodsdon was invaluable with his insight on engineering and my sisters, Stephanie Faulkner, Seresa Morgan, and Rachel Thomas, offered suggestions and insights from their own careers in accounting and finance. My parents and family were supportive and put up with my absences while I finished the manuscript. Finally, I must offer special thanks to Denis Garrett, who formatted much of this book and kept me going with her great sense of humor and her wealth of knowledge from her life experiences, and to Larry, who lived this experience from start to finish, and remains the world's best husband.

Contents

Chapter 7

Chapter 8

Chapter 9

Chapter 10

Chapter 11

Chapter 12

CONTENTS

Introduction

S O YOU WANT A PROFESSIONAL OR EXECUTIVE JOB: WELCOME TO the world of temping.

Are you a successful executive who is between jobs? Are you an accountant, engineer, lawyer, doctor, information technology specialist, or healthcare provider? Did you know that someone with your knowledge and skills can make a lot more money working for a staffing service than as a full-time employee of a company? Do you have marketable skills that are in demand by many businesses today? Do you need a place to work?

Are you a casualty of a changing corporate world, or just changing your personal expectations? In other words, are you looking for another position because of a buyout, corporate takeover, job elimination, downsizing, or outsourcing? Do you need a way to network yourself into another professional job and have an income at the same time? Did you know you can do that by temping?

Have you been asked to retire early? Have you been made an offer you cannot refuse and forced to leave a job that you thought was secure? Are you at a point where you do not know where to go next and you need money?

Do you need to work flexible hours rather than a standard nine-to-five schedule? Do you want to have more control of the quality of your life and not feel as though you are owned by the people you work for? Temping gives you the flexibility to interview for a professional, executive, or administrative position and earn money at the same time.

If you answered yes to any of these questions, then read on about the opportunities for professionals of working as temps.

Today, staffing services frequently label professional technical temps as "consultants," and some call them "associates." That is because staffing services want to now reach out beyond those they have traditionally put to work in the past, office and factory workers. For the purposes of this book, we will refer to temporary employees who are executives, managers, computer experts, scientists, doctors, nurses, engineers, lawyers, paralegals, and accountants as professional technical temps and sometimes just as temps.

Welcome to the changing workforce. The temporary employment industry is the second-fastest-growing industry in the world (second only to the computer industry). The industry has grown because companies are changing the way they hire workers. Temporary employees are a part of getting the job done today in everything from very small businesses to Fortune 500 companies. According to the National Association of Temporary and Staffing Services (NATSS), professionals are the fastest-growing type of temporary workers. Three years ago, *Working Woman* magazine listed professional temp placement as one of the 25 hottest careers in the United States as they reported that the use of professional temps was increasing four times faster than any other aspect of temp personnel.

National Business Employment Weekly has published four issues in the last two years specifically for the professional temp, because that is such a hot industry and there is so much demand for information about it.

No longer can someone earn a college degree, prepare for a field, work for a company, and expect to stay there for the next 20 years. When you enter the workforce today you can expect to change jobs or employers up to five times.

There is no permanent job security, even for professionals. People entering the workforce see mid- and upper-level management being outplaced or downsized by companies where they have worked for 10 and 20 years. As a result, people no longer typically start work at a particular company and plan to retire there.

This book is designed as a career path for professionals, executives, administrators, accountants, attorneys, doctors, nurses, human resources specialists, computer systems analysts, information technology specialists, marketing experts, business consultants, and others who want to or need to work temp and need more information as to how the temporary employment industry works. It is based on my 10 years in the temporary staffing service business and based on a 1997 survey I have made of staffing services and professional employment opportunities in Atlanta, Boston, Chicago, Cincinnati, Fort Worth, Los Angeles, Miami, New Orleans, New York City, Salt Lake City, San Francisco, Seattle, and Washington, DC. Read on to learn what a professional or executive temporary employee is, how employment staffing services work, and how to make the temporary employment industry work for you.

CHAPTER ONE

"Temp" Is Not a Dirty Word

IN THE 1950S THE TEMP INDUSTRY WAS VIEWED AS A SERVICE PRO-viding clerical and secretarial help on a daily or weekly basis when a regular employee was out sick or on vacation. No more. The modern economy is now service-oriented; the workforce has evolved from an industrial-based workforce to one that is service-based. The temporary employment business has changed from just being able to send out secretaries and factory workers to being a staffing service that provides professional, executive, and administrative help on both a short-term and a long-term basis. The staffing service has prospered. As the postwar economy evolved, the major national temping services also evolved—so much so that they formed their own professional association and renamed themselves as staffing services.

The National Association of Temporary and Staffing Services or NATSS estimates there are more than two million temporary employees working in the American economy each and every day. And more than five million people work as temporary employees at some point during an average year. Approximately one-half of these temps are professional and administrative staff.

There are more than 35 million professional, executive, and managerial employees in the United States, according to *National Business Employment Weekly*, and the U.S. Bureau of Labor Statistics reports that 7.7% of them or 2.7 million people are working temporary staffing positions. What does this mean? It means more opportunity for you, the prospective professional technical temp, to earn more as a temp.

Professionals and executives temp for many different reasons: to achieve flexibility in their personal lives (these temps probably will never work at permanent jobs); to gain experience and network while they are hunting for permanent employment; because they are raising young children at home or caring for elderly parents and cannot work a full-time schedule; because they have been "outplaced" or let go from their employment and have not yet succeeded in finding new permanent work; to supplement their income; to keep up their contacts and interest in their profession when they are retired or semiretired; and finally because they are awaiting licensing or certification by appropriate regulatory services or boards.

From the point of view of the client company who engages the assistance of a professional staffing service, there are many and varied reasons why they need or want to employ professional temps.

First, usually companies can save about 50% of their personnel costs since they do not have to pay benefits or payroll taxes. In other words, the true cost of an employee for a company can be calculated as in Figure 1.1.

Second, technical and professional businesses require specific expertise, and when the demand for engineers, lawyers, accountants, healthcare professionals, and computer specialists is high, it may be nearly impossible to locate and retain that expertise from an employee on a full-time basis.

Third, when a company has a specific contract or work project with a fixed termination date, it may be preferable to add to professional staff through the use of temps since that overhead expense will cease on the fixed date when the contract expires.

Fourth, despite all the efforts, no one has yet succeeded in repealing the business cycle. Thus, most companies are still subject to boom-and-bust swings. During the peak boom years they need to staff up quickly and will resort to the use of professional temps during those times.

In an article titled "An Inside Look at Executive Temping" in the March 9, 1997, issue of *National Business Employment Weekly*, a poll of 416 vice presidents and human resources directors reported 36%

FIGURE 1.1   The True Cost of a Professional Technical Temp

Company/Position Comparison

Hourly rate ($) × 40 hours per week × 52 weeks	$
Annual overtime pay (number of hours × 1.5 × $ hourly pay)	$
Annual bonus pay or incentive pay	$
Total annual salary:	$

Taxes

FICA at 7.65% of annual salary	$
State unemployment at 1.5% of annual salary	$
Federal unemployment at .8% of annual salary	$
Workers' compensation at 5% of annual salary	$

Insurance	$
Group medical/life insurance at $ per month × 12 months	$
Dental policy at $ per month × 12 months	$
401(k) plan/pension	$
Hiring recruitment and payrolling cost at 10% first-year salary	$
Total annual salary ($) divided by 2080 hours per year = cost per hour	$
Vacation at hours × $	$
Holidays at hours × $	$
Sick leave at hours × $	$

Other: does not include cost of W/C injury, turnover, legal cost
of any hiring liabilities, administrative headaches, or cost
of money

Total annual salary and fringe benefits:	$
$ total annual salary and fringe benefits ÷ 2080 hours = total hourly rate	$

Compared to a Staffing Service

Total hourly rate for a professional technical temp	$
Hourly savings	$
Annual savings: number of people × $ × 2080 hours	$

used white-collar temps for accounting, legal, marketing, human resources, information systems, and administrative functions.

According to the Bureau of Labor Statistics' analysis of professional temps, the average hourly salary of professional temps is $24.11. That's an average of almost $1000 per week. *National Busi-*

ness Employment Weekly also reports that "for senior executives, turn-around specialists, and top computer programmers, annual earnings typically reach six figures." Thus, a professional temp can earn $50,000 to $100,000 per year.

Another recent study of more than 400 companies conducted for Olsten Corporation, one of the world's largest staffing services, documents that more than one-third of the surveyed companies regularly employ professional executives and managers on a temporary basis for legal, accounting, computer, marketing, and managerial jobs. That means a lot of opportunity for you, the professional technical temp.

In an interview, Tony Lee, editor of *National Business Employment Weekly*, said his biggest surprise was that so many qualified professionals who are looking for work have not discovered or considered the bonanza of available jobs and money that is out there for them in temping. Lee said people still think temping is just for secretaries, day laborers, and factory workers. His research has shown that those who are most computer literate are most at ease at being a professional temp. Other professionals must still get used to the concept. The readership of *National Business Employment Weekly* is made up of middle- to senior-level executives who are accustomed to earning $50,000 annually. In fact, his publication has used the term *interim executive* instead of professional technical temp to educate readers about what a temp really is and the advantage of using the staffing industry to market professional technical skills.

Lee also said there are three groups of people in the higher-income temp bracket today. The first group consists of people who have had trouble finding a job. They have been looking for work and will sign up with a professional staffing service because they must have immediate income. These people view temping as a last resort and will quit temping in a minute if they are offered any full-time or permanent job. They view temping as a real comedown in their professional growth and feel that any full-time job is better than a temporary one.

For example, Jack worked as an information technology specialist at a company that was acquired by another company. As a result, Jack lost his job. Jack looked for work while living off his severance package.

After that ran out, Jack signed up with a staffing service who placed people with his skills on temporary jobs. The staffing service offered Jack a choice of jobs. One of these paid a lot of money and would last several months, but there was no question but that it was an interim job with no chance of being permanent. Another job was a temp-to-hire where a company would try out a temp and, if satisfactory, would then hire that person at the end of three months. Even though the temp-to-hire job paid less money than the other job, Jack took it because emotionally he needed the security of a so-called permanent job.

The second group in the higher-income temp bracket consists of those who are professional technical temps, according to Lee, and will use temporary work as a way to change careers. Lee gives the example of someone who has worked as an accountant for several years but really wants to be in public relations. The accountant quits a full-time job at an accounting firm and signs up with an accounting staffing service, asking to be placed on jobs in PR firms that require accounting skills. The staffing service places him on a six-month assignment doing financial analysis for a PR firm where he gets to demonstrate and gain income from his accounting skills and learn about public relations at the same time. That person does the job so well that by the end of six months he has become indispensable. The accountant used temping as a way to work himself into a dream job of being a part of a PR firm.

The third group of professional temps, according to Lee, are those who want the flexibility of interim work. They view themselves as a cut above the regular permanent employee. They will sign up for project work and work a 70-hour week one week, knowing when they finish the 70 hours they can have the next week off to travel or do whatever they want to do with their time.

CHAPTER TWO

Staffing Services versus Headhunters versus Independent Contractors

Temporary Employee or "Temp" Defined

A TEMPORARY EMPLOYEE IS SOMEONE WHO IS NOT A PERMANENT employee. In fact, the dictionary says something that is temporary is the opposite of what is permanent. As mentioned in the Introductuion, for the purposes of this book, professional, executive, or administrative temporary employees will be called temps.

People who work in a business who are not part of the permanent or full-time workforce are called part-time workers or temps. Businesses may have their own pool of temps or they may hire a temporary employment service or staffing service to send temps to them. A staffing service will be defined later in this chapter.

Permanent employees are people who are hired to be a lasting or continuous part of a company. A company hires them for an indefinite amount of time. When a permanent employee leaves a company, it is usually because the employee has taken another job, is retiring, is moving, or has been fired.

Businesses are in existence to provide a service or sell a product. They must have staff to do this. Businesses now have two ways of creating a staff. They can do it the standard way, which is to create their own personnel department. The personnel or human resources department then hires people or staff to be permanent employees for that particular company. Those people may stay and be promoted and grow with the company—that is, if they work out.

If these permanent employees do not work out, the business must fire them and start the recruitment process all over again. That keeps the personnel office of the company busy.

Or the company may choose to hire staff in another way: The company may contract with a staffing service to send temps over to the business. These temps will do the same work that full-time employees do, but the business where the temps work is not responsible for providing benefits (health insurance, a retirement plan, etc.) for them. And, if the temporary employee is not a good fit for the business where he or she is working, it is the problem of the temp service to fix it, not the problem of the personnel department of the business. As temporary or staffing services work with more sophisticated or professional employees, the nature of the relationship between the service and the temps is changing. Services are offering better benefits to get the most qualified pool of employees.

Growth of Professional Technical Temps

PROFESSIONAL TEMPS ARE THOSE SKILLED IN THE FINANCIAL AND legal fields as well as the occupations of information technology, computer science, engineering, healthcare, management, and related fields. The financial professionals include accountants, auditors, chief financial officers, and bookkeepers. The legal professionals who temp are paralegals and attorneys. People who are in science and healthcare, sales and marketing professionals, and those in middle and senior management are also doing professional temping. In fact, according to NATSS, the use of professional temporaries has increased 48% from 1991 through 1996. Professional and technical staffing increased 25% annually, according to *Staffing Industry Review*, August 1996.

One of the fastest-growing segments of temp skills includes technical workers. These are engineers, computer programmers, computer systems analysts, designers, draftspersons, and technical illustrators and editors.

The nature of the staffing service has changed. It was previously known as a business of sending the right secretary or laborer to fill in for some day needs.

Now the temporary industry calls itself the staffing service industry because the industry is no longer just about temping. The staffing industry is about finding skills and matching them to the demands of businesses. Therefore, the staffing industry has evolved from sending only factory workers and secretaries to placing people who have sophisticated professional technical skills. That is why the fastest-growing segment of temporary usage is professional temporaries. Temp services or staffing services now send people on jobs who are information technology specialists.

Professional Temp Defined

PROFESSIONAL TECHNICAL TEMPS MAY BE LICENSED BY REGULATORY services or the government to practice their profession (attorneys, doctors, accountants, engineers); their work is subject to a professional code of ethics; and they almost always hold academic degrees. Professional temps are not in the traditional occupations noted for hiring temps, such as office support, secretaries, and factory workers. Examples of professional temps are architects, physician assistants, registered nurses, licensed practical nurses, pharmacists, lawyers, paralegals, engineers, and accountants.

Executive Temp Defined

THE EXECUTIVE TEMP TENDS TO HAVE EXPERIENCE IN MANAGEMENT and supervision of others and skills for long-range planning and implementation of company goals. Examples are city planner, executive vice president, sales manager, and product manager.

Technical Temp Defined

THE TECHNICAL TEMP MAY OR MAY NOT HOLD AN ACADEMIC DEGREE, but through job experience or life skills has acquired a particular job-related talent that benefits from the temp's knowledge. Examples are systems analysts, computer software architects, information system and computer consultants, computer programmers, graphic artists, and technical writers.

Professional, executive, and technical temps make up almost one-fourth of the temporary workforce, according to the National Association of Temporary and Staffing Services (NATSS). This segment is expected to remain the fastest-growing segment of the staffing industry. What that means to you, the professional technical temp, is that now is an opportune time for you to enter the world of temping.

Why Do Businesses Use Temps?

THE WORKFORCE HAS CHANGED OVER THE PAST 20 YEARS. FEW WORKERS spend their lives at the same company anymore, and companies are quicker to downsize at the first sign of problems. These changes are because of growth, downsizing, buyouts, takeovers, technology, people living and working longer, and companies going out of business.

What does this mean to you? It means more and more people have to be flexible to work. Companies must be more flexible to hire good people. Not everything is a nine-to-five job, and there is no security in the job market as there was in the past. Being a good employee and being loyal will not guarantee job security.

Businesses still need to get the work done. They want to cut their costs and not be responsible for the financial security of all of their workers. So they turn to staffing services to provide the workers.

History of the Temporary Employment Industry

YEARS AGO TEMPORARY STAFFING SERVICES WERE CALLED FOR PRImarily office jobs. These jobs were mostly secretarial in nature and were predominately filled by women. These temps were homemakers who did not want to work full-time outside the home or mothers who were reentering the workforce after spending time at home raising their children. Other temps were people between jobs who used temporary work to make money until they found another job. Still other temps were people who were new to a community and wanted to work temp while they looked for a permanent position.

Temporary staffing services sent these temps to businesses both large and small who needed secretaries for one day or several weeks. Occasionally businesses hired these temps because they were in the job when there was a full-time opening and the temp was in the right place at the right time.

As the workforce and businesses changed, the type of people who temped changed. People with skills that were not secretarial started temping. More men started temping. Computers changed the way office work was done, and people who had capabilities other than the traditional secretarial skills entered the temp workforce.

The temporary employment business has grown as a result. Companies save money by using temps. The companies that contract with staffing services do not have to provide for temps what they must provide for permanent employees, like health insurance, vacation pay, and retirement programs.

What Is a Staffing Service?

FOR THE PURPOSES OF THIS BOOK, A TEMPORARY EMPLOYMENT SERvice will be called a staffing service. A staffing service is defined as a company that recruits people (temporaries) who are looking for work, then places them in temporary part-time or full-time jobs.

Those who work for the staffing service are called temporary employees or, out there in the job world, temps.

In my hometown there are more than 70 companies listed in the yellow pages under the heading of employment services/staffing services. Many of these staffing services specialize in areas like general office, clerical, legal, accounting, sales, engineering, medical, industrial, warehouse, or factory placement.

Why Use a Staffing Service?

PEOPLE SIGN UP OR REGISTER WITH A SERVICE TO FIND A TEMPORARY or permanent job and get paid. A staffing service will do the work of finding the job for the people who temp for them. This saves people the time of going out and finding a job themselves.

What kind of jobs do temps do? A person can work temp in many capacities in many types of environments. For instance, in an office temps can do everything from programming computers, to supervising an accounting division, to managing projects, to acting as the temporary CEO! The days when a temp did only the work no one else wanted to do or was limited to strictly secretarial work are gone.

Temping is a great way to get your foot in the door of many companies, gain experience, and get paid while you are doing it.

Why Are Staffing Services Here and What Do They Do?

STAFFING SERVICES WERE ESTABLISHED TO FILL A NEED FOR MANY companies. Businesses have to get the work done, but do not always know how many people it will take to accomplish objectives. Some companies that use temps use them for special seasonal projects. They do not want these people listed in their head count or permanent employee count all year long, so they hire temps for a few days, weeks, or months at a time.

Some businesses do not have a personnel or human resources office and use staffing services to do all of their recruiting, interviewing, screening, and reference checking. Services then send candidates for the final selection to businesses who may conduct the concluding interview and select personnel for their companies through these pools of people. A staffing service does all the work a regular personnel department would do and takes the initial risk by screening and selecting the most qualified applicants for a job.

Who Hires Temps?

BUSINESSES LIKE SILICON VALLEY COMPUTER COMPANIES, GENERAL Motors, Citibank, Federal Express, NYNEX, AT&T, Microsoft, Netscape, and Opryland USA have called staffing services for special projects, for short-term jobs, or to fill very specialized jobs when they haven't been able to find the people themselves. Many of these people have only been there for a short period of time as a temp. Others happened to be at the right place at the right time and were hired as full-time employees of the businesses where they started work as a temp.

Other companies use staffing services to covertly find people they do not want to openly advertise and recruit for. This type of recruitment can be done for all types of jobs, including engineers, accountants, and chief financial officers (CFOs).

Headhunters

STAFFING SERVICES THAT SPECIALIZE IN EXECUTIVE RECRUITMENT OR highly paid positions are often called headhunters. These people recruit and place candidates all over the world and operate from a who-you-know format. For example, if a headhunter or executive placement company is hired by XYZ Corporation to find an industrial engineer, the headhunter will search through the resumes on file for an industrial engineer.

If the headhunter company does not have any qualified industrial engineers on file, they will call companies that have industrial engineers working for them, and ask engineers there if they know anyone who would be interested in the job the headhunter is trying to fill.

What the headhunter wants is for the person who takes the call to be interested or to refer the headhunter to other industrial engineers who are interested.

Outplacement Firms or Career Transition Services

IN THE PAST, OUTPLACEMENT FIRMS HAD THE REPUTATION OF HELPING those who did not fit in their jobs. People who were sent to outplacement firms might have been unfairly viewed as losers because they did not fit in one environment and were let go. Companies who fired or let people go sent them to these outplacement firms to be improved so that other companies would hire these people. That has changed.

These companies now call themselves career transition services. They now try to help people who have changed jobs. They may have changed jobs because they were fired, were downsized, or simply walked away from a job they no longer liked. Now firms that were called outplacement firms in the past try to help these people make a transition to jobs where they will be a better fit. The world of temping can be a productive avenue for such people.

Jerry L. Thomas is CEO/senior consultant for The Strickland Group, a career transition service, and has many years of experience working with people in transition. The Strickland Group works with high-level executives and helps them with transitions and coaching for future employment. Thomas said The Strickland Group tries to help people with an effective job service campaign. This campaign helps people in terms of "skills, values, and interests." The Strickland Group examines clients' technical and human skills, and then people decide what they should do next. Is it retirement or another job? The next job can now be found through executive temping! Outplacement firms and career transition services are looking for success stories from staffing services that are placing the professional technical temp on jobs.

In the past, people like Thomas have not viewed temping as an option for the people with white-collar executive skills who come to The Strickland Group for guidance. That is because companies like The Strickland Group saw temping as being for those who had secretarial skills or wanted to work in a factory. Since the fastest-growing segment of the temp or staffing industry is now the professional technical area, companies like The Strickland Group could now refer their candidates to staffing services.

Contract Positions

MOST STAFFING SERVICES AS WE KNOW THEM TODAY ARE PERSONNEL services that place people on one-day to indefinite-duration job assignments. However, the Internal Revenue Service (IRS) has a very specific definition of what an independent contractor is and how that position affects payroll taxes. Refer to the sections on independent contractors starting at page 23.

How Do Staffing Services Make Their Money?

STAFFING SERVICES ARE EITHER EMPLOYEE- OR EMPLOYER-PAID SER-vices. If you use a staffing service to find temporary or permanent work, that means you, the temp, are the employee of the staffing service. A temp never should pay a staffing service to find the temp a job, so stay away from staffing services that are employee-paid staffing services or that charge you money for finding you work. You want to use a staffing service that is employer-paid. That means the staffing service charges the business where they place you a fee for finding a temp for the business.

Do not use employee-paid fee staffing services. They will charge you a fee for finding you a temporary or permanent job. There are too many employer-paid staffing services that want you that will not charge you a fee. Stay away from the ones that charge you money to find you a job.

The businesses that hire the staffing services should be the ones that pay for the service, not you, the professional technical temp.

There is a mistaken perception that all staffing services will charge temps a fee to find them a job. That is not correct, and you should avoid staffing services that do charge the temp a fee. Go only to the staffing services that pay you, the temp, not the staffing services that would charge the temp money for finding work.

An employer-paid service will charge the business where they place a temporary employee an hourly rate for filling that job. That rate is figured in two basic steps. Part one includes the essential required items of any person's hourly pay, such as the actual hourly pay rate plus taxes, Social Security, bond, and workers' compensation.

The second part of the rate is where staffing services make their money. After figuring what they have to pay someone per hour, the staffing service will add to that a markup or cost that allows the staffing service to make money. They will charge a business enough per hour so that the staffing service makes a profit. The staffing service is like any other business: It must make a profit to stay in business. The staffing service has to pay its own employees and cover its other business expenses. The staffing service will charge the business anywhere from 30% to 50% more per hour than whatever they are paying their temp. If you, the temp, are paid $20 an hour, the staffing service is probably billing the business where you are working $26 to $30 an hour.

Remember that the employer-paid staffing service will charge a fee to the business where the temporary employee works, not to the temporary employee.

Staffing services are in business to make money, so they must include in each hourly rate money that will cover their overhead (e.g., their rent, salaries of their staff) and a percentage of margin for their profit. A bank that hires the same person for the same job must factor in not only the person's salary, but the cost of providing health and retirement benefits.

A company's staff person whose annual salary is $50,000 not only costs the company $50,000 but also costs an additional 30%, or $15,000, in benefits. Benefits would include vacation and sick pay and a retirement fund. The temporary industry has grown because companies, by paying an hourly rate to a staffing service, can get the right skill, can get the job done, and do not have to be responsible for unemployment or benefits for these people.

Flat Fees versus Hourly Fees

SOME COMPANIES PAY A STAFFING SERVICE A FLAT FEE FOR LOCATING persons for them, rather than the 30% to 50% markup of hourly fees. This flat fee is usually based on the percentage of an annual salary, often 20% to 30%. For example, if a person is placed on a job at $40,000, the staffing service will charge the business hiring the person a percentage of that $40,000 (20% to 30% of the salary would be $8000 to $12,000). Some headhunters can make a very good income from charging percentages of executive salaries. A 25% fee for someone making $75,000 is $18,750. A few placements like that each year can add up to a lot of money.

As stated previously, an employee-paid staffing service will charge the temporary employees a percentage of their salary for finding them a job. There are many staffing services that make their money by charging the businesses where they place temps. It makes sense to stay away from those who charge the temps money for finding them the jobs.

Read Before You Sign a Contract

MAKE SURE YOU KNOW THE DIFFERENCE BETWEEN AN EMPLOYER- AND an employee-paid staffing service before signing anything. Otherwise, you could end up with a bad experience. Denise did.

Denise was very anxious to get away from her current job as an accountant. She had excellent skills and signed up with the first staffing service she found. The staffing service quickly sent her to an office for an interview. The office called the staffing service and said they wanted to hire Denise. Denise signed a contract with the staffing service and accepted the job. What Denise did not take the time to find out was that she agreed to pay the staffing service 10 percent of her first year's income at the new job and that she must stay on the job at least a year or have to pay a penalty fee to the staffing service. As a result, Denise paid a lot of money and worked at a job she did not like.

Had Denise taken the time to do some investigating, she would have found several staffing services that would not have charged her anything to find her a temporary or full-time job. She had excellent skills and could have had more jobs to choose from than the first job she accepted.

Headhunters or professional recruiting services can work the same way. They are going to make their money somewhere, so make sure you know the type you are using before you sign anything. Many companies will only pay a headhunter for an experienced candidate. Those with little or no experience, like recent graduates or those changing fields, may not be viewed by headhunters as attractive candidates since they are hard to place.

So what is a staffing service? A company that makes its money matching people with jobs. They are going to make their money from either the people they place or the businesses who hire them. Know the difference when selecting a staffing service.

Where the Professional Technical Temps Work

TEMPS WORK EVERYWHERE, SINCE TEMPS CAN DO ANY JOB FROM working in a factory to running a company. All types of companies hire temps. The next section is a summary of a few of the types of businesses where temps work today.

Temping is a good way to get your foot in the door and gain experience at the same time. Many times people are turned down for jobs because they lack experience. If they get in somewhere as a temp and do a good job they make a good impression. Temps who make a good impression may be recommended for openings for full-time jobs where they have worked as a temp. Or, someone may advise the temp of a similar job in another company and put in a good word for the temp because of the excellent job the person has done temping.

What kinds of businesses use temps? Here are several examples. Subsequent chapters discuss different types of professions that temp and the businesses where temps work.

Banks

Banks use temps in most of their departments. These temps work as temporary personnel recruiters, executive assistants, lawyers, paralegals, auditors, and accountants. Some banks will train their professional technical temps and some ask for very specific qualifications like experience reconciling statements, writing legal opinion letters, conducting title searches, or working on various types of software as an information technology specialist.

Hospitals and Healthcare Companies

Hospitals are big businesses and use professional technical temps for everything from temporary chief executive officers (CEOs) to administrators, accountants, auditors, information technology specialists, claims administrators, nurses, doctors, and medical technicians. Hospitals are very competitive, and the government is trying to force healthcare companies to become more cost-effective. The number of employees in healthcare may fluctuate. healthcare companies hire lots of professional technical temps for special projects, job vacancies, vacation coverage, or coverage for medical leave.

Many hospitals offer excellent benefits, so they are a popular industry to choose if benefits are important. Knowledge of the medical or nursing professions and Medicare as well as experience with the insurance industry is very helpful when working temp in healthcare.

Healthcare companies also hire professional technical temps in a variety of fields. Some hire temps who are professional physician recruiters; others may be accountants or lobbyists. There is a demand for the most current skills in information technology or computer knowledge. They also hire traditional accountants, lawyers, and paralegals. Many healthcare companies are turning to the staffing industry to find people who have skills in areas of science. Some healthcare companies are turning over areas of research to a staffing service to find and supervise those skilled in various aspects of science.

The Legal Profession

Law offices use professional technical temps who are lawyers, paralegals, and legal assistants. Most temps who are proficient in legal terminology or who have had legal experience can work just about anytime they want to. Some law offices have their own pools of temps who are lawyers or paralegals that they employ in-house. This is to make sure information within these law firms is kept confidential.

Accounting

Accounting is a specific skill that has become very popular in the temporary industry. There are lots of staffing services that specialize and place temps only in accounting jobs. These jobs can be everything from basic data entry on accounting programs and bookkeeping to a very specialized form of accounting that requires an experienced auditor, a certified public accountant (CPA), or a chief financial officer (CFO). Staffing services that do accounting work are especially busy during tax season or in the months leading up to March 15, April 15, and June 30.

Temps who have accounting skills can work in many types of industries, from tax firms to healthcare to entertainment. Every business relies on someone to take care of their documents relating to profit and loss, but not every business needs accounting or bookkeeping employees to work for them 52 weeks a year. Therefore, businesses both large and small have turned to staffing services to provide the skills for their accounting needs.

Insurance

Insurance firms use temps for systems analysis, computer programming, property management, training, customer service, and human resources work.

Medical Practices

Doctors' offices also use temps for everything from doctors to nurses to physician assistants. Another skill that is helpful for working in a medical practice is experience with insurance companies. Some technicians and nurses now work as temps because it gives them more flexibility in their schedules.

Engineering Firms

People who work in engineering firms need technical skills. Today people who temp in these firms are engineers, architects, and draftspersons. Many of these people combine computer skills with special skills needed to be engineers. The more computer knowledge you have, the better your chances are to be a successful professional technical temp in jobs relating to engineering.

Laboratories

Laboratories hire temps. It is important to get a detailed job description when working in a lab because of the type of work they do. Laboratories hire temps with technical scientific skills as well as those who know accounting.

Universities or Colleges

Many universities use temps all over their campuses. Some even have their own temporary services. Temps at colleges often perform special projects for the college or for each university department.

Computer Companies

The computer industry is growing so fast that many computer companies hire temps just to keep up with their business or to be able to staff their initial start-ups and help desks. Of course, if you want to work with computers as a professional technical temp you must have computer knowledge. As a temp, you could work in a specific area that requires knowledge of a certain type of computer programming or use more wide-ranging information technology skills. Working as a temp for any computer company would be a great way to gain experience in today's fast-growing world of information technology.

Companies That Move

Companies that have just relocated or are brand-new frequently use staffing services. New companies are not sure how many employees will be needed. Instead of starting out with too many employees, these new companies will hire temps to get the work done. Many temps who work with new companies have an excellent chance of becoming full-time or permanent employees of the company because they will have already proved they are qualified for the job.

Businesses who relocate from one city to another also use a lot of temps. This is because the companies are often not sure how many of their employees will relocate. Until their full-time employees make a decision about relocation, a company will use temps to get the work done. If a temp is doing the job of an employee who chooses not to relocate, the temp will be in a good position to apply for a job with that company.

Communications

Companies in the cellular communications business have used temps for opening many departments, because the industry has grown so fast and companies have been sure to create departments for the different types of cellular services they sell. They use temps in customer service to plan strategies for customer problems as well as engineers and information technology experts to do surveys about future needs.

Sales and Marketing

Both inside and outside sales positions may be filled by temps. Many marketing and research companies use temps for training, recruitment, personnel, human resources, and computer applications positions. Some companies will pay a fee to a staffing service to find qualified sales or marketing people. Make sure if you want to work as a professional temp in sales that you do your research and find a staffing service that is qualified to place you in a sales position. In other words, ask the staffing service for stories of success where the staffing service has found jobs for those in sales so that you will not waste your time working with a staffing service that cannot or will not ever be able to place you in a sales job.

Government and Politics

Lobbying groups and political organizations hire temps. Many of these jobs are project work or support jobs. Temps may do survey work or help organize campaigns. Many political organizations turn to staffing services to fill their accounting positions because they have a hard time finding people with specific skills like accounting who want to work in politics.

Even government uses temps. Many government agencies are under what is called a hiring freeze and are not able to hire additional staff. Government gets around such hiring freezes by using temps and not adding them to their permanent head count.

Public Relations

There are not very many public relations firms that use staffing services to find people to work for them, because PR firms are usually flooded with resumes of people looking for jobs. They rarely turn to staffing services to help them fill full-time jobs. They will call staffing services for temps to meet unexpected needs such as the need for a skilled computer person or an accountant to work on a special project. If you really want to work in a business like this, you may be able to use staffing services to get your foot in the door.

Entertainment

The entertainment industry is a lot like PR firms. Firms that are in the film, recording, music, and publishing businesses are also flooded with resumes. However, they call staffing services for support positions. These support positions are critical to the entertainment industry, and staffing services only send very qualified temps.

In my hometown of Nashville, Tennessee, it has been my experience that you could starve while you wait for a temp job in the entertainment industry. My advice is to make your preference known to the staffing services with whom you work. Tell them that you want to work in the entertainment industry if that is what you really want to do. In Nashville, the music industry will call a staffing service for a specific job to be done, and specialists in the area of information technology are sometimes sought. The music business in Nashville does not want a staffing service to send in a temp who wants to be an entertainer. If that happens, the staffing service will not be called again. There are stories of country music stars such as Wynonna Judd and Tracy Lawrence (and Garth Brooks's wife) who worked as temps while they were trying to make it in the country music business, but these stories are few and far between.

There are many professionals who run the business of entertainment, from information technology specialists to accountants to lawyers. If you have any of these skills and are good with people, call the particular entertainment business where you want to work, and ask to be referred to a staffing service they use. Sign up with that staffing service and ask to be placed at the entertainment business. In the meantime, be flexible and take other temp jobs to make ends meet.

If a company moves to your city and you want to work for that company, find out what staffing service they are using and apply with that staffing service. Then ask the staffing service to send you to that company.

The Difference between Independent Contractors and Professional Technical Temps

DO YOU WANT TO BE IN BUSINESS FOR YOURSELF? BE RESPONSIBLE FOR funding your own health and life insurance? Be responsible for withholding your own taxes, making sure you are allocating from each paycheck what needs to go to Uncle Sam? Do you want to have the sole responsibility for planning and funding your own retirement plan? Do you want to seek out those who need your services and constantly sell yourself? If so, you may want to be an independent contractor. There is a big difference between the professional technical temp and the independent contractor. The independent contractor wants to do all of the aforementioned chores and enjoys all the headaches associated with them. The professional technical temp would rather use his or her technical skills and let someone else—a staffing service—deal with finding the jobs and all the details with the government and retirement planning that go along with these jobs.

Employee or Independent Contractor?

EMPLOYEE OR INDEPENDENT CONTRACTOR—WORKERS HAVE TO BE one or the other. Workers who should be classified as employees but are not may be losing out on workers' compensation, unemployment benefits, and, in many cases, group insurance (including life and health) and retirement benefits.

Many people are wrongly labeled as independent contractors when they are really employees. These mislabeled workers are found in every occupation. However, no matter how an employer labels you, it is wise to determine for yourself if you are what your employer says you are.

If you have an employer-employee relationship, it doesn't matter whether you're called an employee, partner, independent contractor, or coadventurer; you're still an employee for tax purposes.

Your employer must withhold income tax on your wages and must pay Social Security tax (FICA), as well as withhold your portion of FICA. Also, your employer is responsible for unemployment tax (FUTA). Each January your employer must give you a Form W-2, "Wage and Tax Statement," showing the amount of taxes withheld the previous year.

If your employer does not withhold and deposit these taxes because you are misclassified, you will not be covered by unemployment compensation or workers' compensation. And you may be hit with a big tax bill at filing time if you have not been credited with paying these taxes during the year through withholding.

In a nutshell, if the person who employs you sets your work hours, provides you with equipment, tells you what to do and how to do it, and can fire you, then chances are you are an employee, not an independent contractor.

It does not matter if the employer allows you freedom of action in your work. What counts is the fact that the employer has the legal right to control the method and result of your work.

At present, the guidelines the Internal Revenue Service (IRS) uses to classify workers is a list of 20 factors regarding the nature of the working relationship. You are probably an employee if several of these factors apply to you (and you should evaluate them both in reference to the staffing service and in reference to the ultimate employer the staffing service sends you to):

- The employer or your supervisor tells you when, where, and how to work.

- The employer trains you to perform services in a particular manner.

- Your services are part of the business operations because they are important to the success of the business.

- Your services are rendered personally.

- The business hires, supervises, and pays workers.

- You have a continuing relationship with the business.

- The business sets your work hours.

- You are required to work or be available full-time.

- You work on the premises of the business, or on a route, or at a location designated by the business.

- You perform services in the order or sequence set by the business.

- You submit regular reports to the business.

- You are paid by the hour, week, or month.

- The business pays your travel and business expenses.

- The business provides your tools, materials, and other equipment.

- You have no significant investment in the business.

- You don't make a profit or suffer a loss from the business.
- You normally work for one business at a time.
- You don't offer your services to the general public.
- The business has the right to fire you.
- You have the right to quit without incurring liability.

Janice is a professional bookkeeper who earns her living keeping books for several small businesses. As an independent contractor, Janice does the bookkeeping work whenever she wants to and submits her fee for services directly to the business. The difference between Janice as an independent contractor and a professional temp is that as a contractor Janice is responsible for finding her clients and determining her time frame of work.

Another important difference is that as an independent contractor, Janice must withhold her own taxes and provide her own benefits. If she were working for a professional staffing service as a temp, the service would find Janice work, withhold her taxes, and often provide her with holiday and health benefits. In order to be successful, independent contractors must have the ability to obtain customers on their own and to be paid for providing a product or service.

To add to this confusion, some companies use special contract workers for specific services. For example, a company may contract out services like landscaping, security, or janitorial services. For the purposes of this book, these types of contracted services and employees will not be addressed.

Many independent contractors consider their contract work to be a part-time job. The Bureau of Labor Statistics says most independent contractors are "more likely to be out of school and have a bachelor's degree." They usually work in professional and administrative areas and are "less likely to work in manufacturing, wholesale, or retail trade."

If someone has the right to control only the result of your work and not the way in which you get that result, then you are probably an independent contractor. For tax purposes, you may receive a

Form 1099-MISC, "Miscellaneous Income," instead of a W-2 from the business hiring you as an independent contractor.

If you're still not sure whether you're an employee or an independent contractor, you can get Publication 937, "Employment Taxes and Information Returns," and Form SS-8, "Determination of Employee Work Status for Purposes of Federal Employment Taxes and Income Tax Withholding." Both are available free from the IRS by calling 1-800-TAX-FORM (1-800-829-3676).

You are responsible for paying your own income tax and self-employment tax. You may want to get Publication 533, "Self-Employment Tax," and Publication 505, "Tax Withholding and Estimated Tax." Both are available free from the IRS.

As an independent contractor, you may have your own employees or you may hire another independent contractor (subcontractor). Get Publication 15, "Circular E, Employer's Tax Guide," and Publication 937 from the IRS to find out what your tax responsibilities are.

The 1099 Route

INDEPENDENT CONTRACTORS ARE OFTEN CONFUSED WITH TRADI-tional temporary technical workers. An independent contractor is a person who usually works for more than one person at a time, who completes projects and goals for an employer in a setting of his or her own choosing rather than the employer's choosing, and who performs the work at the time the worker picks rather than when the employer chooses.

The contractor usually sends a bill directly to the person for whom the work was done. The contractor is responsible for paying his or her own taxes and benefits. That means the contractor has to set up a system of withholding taxes and, if desired, benefits like health and life insurance and a retirement plan. The generation of baby boomers (those born between 1945 and 1964) are concerned about whether Social Security will be around when they get ready to retire, so they feel they had better do their own retirement planning.

Things like 401(k) plans and mutual funds are part of the everyday verbiage of today's professional temp and independent contractor.

Those who have marketable skills, which are a characteristic of today's successful white-collar temp, will find they have a lot of options to choose from as they decide which staffing service to work through. What are the things that the professional temp should look for? The temp should pick the service that will pay the most money and offer the most benefits and that will best fit the lifestyle and needs of the temp.

Let's take the example of Martha, a creative writer. Martha worked for a government agency from the time she graduated from a prestigious university in the mid-1960s until 1997. Her agency decided to offer special packages to those who had more than 30 years of service in order to try to get some of the employees to take early retirement, as government departments will do.

Martha weighed her options and decided to take the government up on their offer of early retirement. But Martha was only 52 years old and was bored as a retiree. She did not want to fill her life with volunteer work, and her family obligations allowed her a lot of flexibility. Martha decided to become an independent contractor and do freelance work.

Martha picked up a lot of work and specialized in writing internal newsletters for corporations. These corporations would hire Martha to develop the stories and get the newsletters published so that they looked professional. Martha did the work from home using a desktop system she set up herself, and subcontracted with a direct mail company that mailed the letters to the addresses she provided.

Martha enjoyed the work very much until it came time to do her taxes. Recordkeeping had never been one of her strong points. When the companies she developed the newsletters for sent her the appropriate 1099 forms she was at a loss as to what to do with them. She ended up paying a CPA a lot of money to do her taxes. All the forms she had to keep up with were a nightmare. As much as Martha enjoyed her work, she was not sure if all the paperwork was worth it until a friend told her about a staffing service he worked for that handled those problems—which brings us to the next topic.

The Trend from Independent Contractors to Pure Technical Staffing Firms

MARTHA VISITED FLEXIBLE PEOPLE STAFFING SERVICE ON THE RECommendation of her friend Michael, who worked there in the field of information technology. He told her this service would pay her a set salary a year, no matter how many or few projects she worked on, and would also provide her with health insurance and stock options. That is what had happened to Michael; it had turned out to be a winwin situation for him.

Michael had chosen this particular staffing service because they recruited and successfully placed information technology specialists and creative writers. When Michael signed on with this service he was told, based on his skills, he would make $62,000 a year. That meant the staffing service would pay him the same amount twice a month, regardless of how many projects, hours, or days he worked for the staffing service, as well as providing him fringe benefits. This was a different concept from the service Michael had previously worked for. The previous staffing service paid him by the hour and did not provide any type of holiday, health, or retirement benefits.

Flexible People Staffing Service offered Michael financial security and peace of mind. These things were important since he was 42 years old, had many more years to work, and had two children to support and educate. The service sent Michael to various cities to install computer software and educate businesses on the type of software that would work best for each business.

During the weeks when Michael did not have an assignment, the staffing service sent him to training classes on the newest and latest tools to be successful in the world of information technology. That was good for both Michael and the staffing service. It meant he was either working or learning new skills. The more skills he learned, the more placeable he was. The more placeable he was, the more he worked. The more he worked, the more money the staffing service made.

Even though others might have considered Michael a professional temp, the staffing service he worked for considered and treated him like a full-time employee. He received an annual salary and all the regular insurance and retirement benefits that most full-time employees receive.

The difference between Michael and independent contractors is that Michael received an annual salary and was not just paid per project the way most independent contractors are. He received health insurance, stock options, 401(k) contributions, and holiday and vacation pay. He did not have separate 1099 forms coming to him from companies he worked for; he received a regular W-2 form from the staffing service.

This trend of providing the best of the best in order to attract professional and technical people to the world of temping or staffing is one that will grow. Staffing services are competing to attract the most skilled people, and thus will compete to offer the best benefits. This is operating outside the norm for many in the traditional world of temping. Many staffing services will pay you, the professional technical temp, the way you want to be paid: by the hour, by the project, or with an annual salary. It all depends on whether you have the skills that are in demand by the staffing services that are competing for the most marketable professional technical temps.

As stated earlier, the increase in the staffing or temp business has been a result of many companies downsizing to save the costs of carrying a large number of employees on their payroll and funding their benefits. The companies have fired people and turned to the staffing industry to hire temps to get the work done. In the past, staffing services did not provide much in the way of benefits to the temp; but that is all changing. Staffing services are now competing to get the most qualified people to work for them. The fastest-growing segment of the temporary industry is the professional technical or white-collar area, and these people will not work for low hourly wages, like many temps in the past have, and they want benefits.

In response to this demand, staffing services are being more and more creative in the benefits they offer. For example, they may pay someone an annual salary as opposed to paying by the project or by the hour. They may offer holiday and sick pay. They may offer the same benefits to the professional technical temps that they offer others at the staffing company, such as the recruiters who place the professional temp on the job. Staffing services are now making stock options and retirement plans available to the professional technical temp as a way of attracting people to work for them.

What Is a Consultant?

MERRIAM-WEBSTER'S COLLEGIATE DICTIONARY, 10TH EDITION, DEfines *consultant* as "one who consults another . . . one who gives professional advice or services." It can sometimes be hard to see the difference between a professional technical temp and a consultant today. In fact, many staffing services who hire professional technical temps call them "consultants," thus adding to the confusion!

The major difference between a consultant and a professional technical temp is that a temp works for a staffing service. A professional technical temp may be called a consultant, but is still employed by or works for the staffing service. A consultant typically works for himself or herself.

Herman Holtz says in his book *How to Succeed as an Independent Consultant* (Third Edition, © 1993, published by John Wiley & Sons, Inc.), "Many independent consultants hire themselves out on the same basis (as technical or professional temporaries), bypassing the job shop or broker." Holtz goes on to say, "Defining yourself as an independent consultant depends primarily on what you choose to be and on what types of assignments or contracts you choose to accept and on how you deliver your services, but not on what you call yourself. In fact, only you can define the term for yourself and what you do."

If you want to know more about becoming a consultant as opposed to a professional technical temp, there are many sources available to choose from. One is *Become a Top Consultant, How the Experts Do It* by Ron Tepper, published by John Wiley & Sons, Inc., in 1985. The book, according to Tepper, "examines 10 of the most successful consultants in the country." Tepper goes on to say, "These 10 are in industries ranging from management consulting and data processing (information systems) to sales training, headhunting, and civil and electrical engineering."

Again, for the purposes of this book, consulting will be treated differently from professional and technical temping. This book is based on the premise that the professional technical temp works for a staffing service and a consultant is self-employed.

Benefits

THERE HAS BEEN A GREAT DEAL IN THE NEWS ABOUT BENEFITS AS they relate to temporary employees. Benefits are the extras people earn on a job in addition to salary: health insurance, life insurance, holiday pay, vacation pay, pension plans, 401(k) plans, tuition reimbursement, merit-awarded raises, and more.

Many people believe the temporary employment industry has grown so rapidly because companies are downsizing and laying off employees in order to avoid paying benefits and therefore save money. Companies still need the work done, so they turn to staffing services to provide the temps. The companies are not responsible for providing benefits to the temps because the temps are not employees of the companies.

Who is responsible for providing the benefits? The staffing services who hire and place the temps on jobs. As more and more people turn to temporary work, benefits are becoming more critical—especially for those professional and technical people who may temp for a long time. Some staffing services are working as a team with businesses that hire temps for long periods of time. The staffing service and the business where the temp works may together offer a special package of benefits to a temp who agrees to stay on a job. The business and the staffing service see this as an added value they can offer the special technical temp to keep the temp from taking his or her skills elsewhere.

Ultimately, it is up to the professional technical temp to decide how important benefits are. Do you, the temp, want to make more per hour so that you can purchase your own benefits, or do you want to work for a staffing service that provides great benefits? Only you can answer.

Staffing services that want to attract the best professional and technical temps will want to offer the most attractive package of benefits. The people they want to place, those with the most sought-after and marketable skills, will want to sign up with the staffing service offering not only the best pay, but also the best benefits.

Unemployment Compensation

PEOPLE WHO SIGN UP OR REGISTER WITH A STAFFING SERVICE USUally cannot turn down a job that is within the scope of their skills and then collect unemployment benefits as an employee of the staffing service. Staffing services keep records of the jobs they offer people, so people are not able to collect from unemployment insurance if they have turned down jobs.

A staffing service could offer a job to someone that did not start right away and if the person turned it down, the person could be in the position to lose unemployment benefits. That means the professional technical temp needs to carefully review the staffing service he or she decides to sign up with and make sure the service is reputable and indeed can provide the jobs at a salary that will compensate the person who may lose a part of a severance package or unemployment insurance as a result of taking a temp job.

CHAPTER THREE

Your Pay as a Professional Technical Temp

THIS CHAPTER GIVES A BRIEF OVERVIEW OF SALARIES FOR white-collar temporaries. A salary compensation breakdown by job description will be provided in later chapters pertaining to specific job categories. A Bureau of Labor Statistics study found that the average professional, executive, or technical temp makes more than $24 an hour and that average compensation is increasing each year.

Most temporary white-collar employees are paid by the hour or by the project. It is very important that you agree with the staffing service as to what your pay will be before accepting any temporary assignment. Also, be aware that whereas traditionally staffing services have not provided any benefits to the temp, some staffing services are beginning to rethink this policy, especially for professional, executive, and administrative temps, and the growing trend in recent years is to provide at least health insurance coverage. Today, some staffing services are offering life insurance, benefit cafeteria plans, and other customary fringe benefits to the professional technical temp.

How do you determine what your pay will be? It is important that you know what your skills are worth on the open market. You should take into consideration your experience and what you have to offer that will make money for the staffing service.

Formula to Determine Pay

TRADITIONALLY, MANY STAFFING SERVICES HAVE USED A STRAIGHT-forward formula to calculate what they will pay their temp employees (Figure 3.1). Staffing services assume there are approximately 40 hours in a workweek. There are 52 weeks in a year. What staffing services do is multiply 40 hours times 52 weeks, which equals 2080 hours. They then divide 2080 hours into what the average annual salary is for the particular profession or occupation, and that determines what the temp will be paid per hour.

Ann had 10 years' experience as an employee relations analyst in Los Angeles when she was downsized; the for-profit hospital where she worked was acquired by a national healthcare provider that already had its own trained staff of employment personnel and human resources professionals such as Ann. At first Ann tried to find full-time employment similar to her old position. She used up her entire severance package while she pursued leads, networked, and even tried a headhunter or executive search firm without success. Then Ann started attending an outplacement clinic course where she met a wide range of consultants, professionals, executives, and administrators much like herself. Several of them remarked about their positive experiences working temp through a staffing service. So Ann decided this kind of work could help update her resume, provide supplemental income, and possibly connect to a wide pool of coworkers

---

FIGURE 3.1 Formula to Determine Pay

Step 1
40 hours × 52 weeks = 2080 hours

Step 2
Annual salary ÷ 2080 hours = hourly wage for temp

Example: If the average annual salary for your profession is $52,000, the usual temp wage would be $25 per hour.

---

and administrators who could lead to other employment; due to the temporary nature of the work, she would still have the freedom to interview for other job positions. She registered with a professional temp firm and was offered a six-month temporary employee relations job assisting the director of a statewide health maintenance organization (HMO).

Ann's annual salary at her old job had been $45,000. She used the formula shown in Figure 3.1 to calculate what her annual salary would have been if she had been paid hourly:

$$\$45,000 \div 2080 = \$21.63$$

Ann also now had to pick up her own benefits that her previous employer had provided. If she were to keep her current lifestyle she would need $26.45 an hour based on benefits costing her over 20% of her income. The staffing service offered her $20 per hour. Ann countered with $25, and they compromised with $22.55. Ann had to make some adjustments in her lifestyle. The staffing service did not offer any employee benefits to its temps, so Ann had to pay for them each month out of her own pocket.

Bureau of Labor Statistics Salary Survey

ACCORDING TO THE MOST CURRENT INFORMATION PROVIDED BY THE U.S. Department of Labor Bureau of Labor Statistics, the average hourly earnings for American temporary professionals range up to $43.05 per hour, depending on field of work. Figure 3.2 lists some average hourly salary rates. These average salaries, for the most part, may have increased by a factor of 4% to 7% since the Bureau of Labor Statistics completed their last study.

Notice then that a professional, executive, or administrative temp who registers with a staffing service and works half a year (1040 hours) on a placement could earn anywhere from $11,000 to $45,000 for only six months' work. For a new entrant to the professional or technical labor force seeking experience and employment, or for someone like Ann who needs to support herself after a corpo-

FIGURE 3.2   Bureau of Labor Statistics Salary Survey

Job Description	Hourly Pay
Doctors	$43.05
Attorneys	$32.70
CPA accountants	$29.15
Computer systems analysts	$28.95
Engineers	$28.75
Computer programmers	$25.40
Human resources specialists	$25.00
Designers	$23.04
Technical writers	$22.71
Commercial graphic artists	$17.63
Non-CPA accountants	$13.96
Drafters	$13.64
Electrical and electronic technicians	$10.32

Source: U.S. Department of Labor, Bureau of Labor Statistics. *Occupational Outlook Handbook, 1996–97 Edition.*

rate downsizing, temping with a staffing service provides an income base plus flexibility and work experience.

Pay

MAKE SURE WHEN YOU ACCEPT YOUR TEMP JOB YOU SAY HOW MUCH you expect to make. Most staffing services will pay by the hour, so be prepared to say what you need to make per hour. There are also services that pay by the project. That means you will be given an assignment to complete for a set amount of money, and you will be paid when the project is completed, no matter how many hours it takes for you to complete it. Be realistic about what you will accept, but do not undersell yourself. Talk to your friends who are working temp and find out what they make. Talk to other temps you meet while you are out on temp assignments and compare salaries. Review the salary wage surveys and see how marketable your skills are.

Jake was an engineer who was referred to Brand X Staffing Service by a friend who had skills similar to Jake's and who had temped for Brand X Staffing Service. Jake knew that his friend was making $32.15 an hour as an engineer, so he put that down as his minimum. He also knew how much he needed to make an hour to meet his goals. He could pay his bills on $32.15 an hour.

If you do not give a service any guidelines on what you need to make, they will tell you what they can pay you. Do not expect to make the same amount per hour as someone whom you met at a full-time job. Typically, temporary workers make less than their full-time counterparts. However, that could change in the future as the value of temporary workers continues to increase in the eyes of those who pay for them.

Don't expect to make $10 an hour stuffing envelopes. You may have had a $40,000 annual salary on your last job, which averages out to $19.23 an hour (to determine your hourly pay, divide your annual salary by 2080, which is 40 hours per week multiplied by 52 weeks; for example, $40,000 divided by 2080 equals $19.23). But, it will be very hard to find temp work that will pay you that $19.23 an hour unless you are placed in your specialized field that involves technical skills like engineering, accounting, or some type of computer programming. There is more and more demand for qualified professional and technical temps, so you may be paid more for the same job by a different staffing service. Pay for the skills of professional technical temps depends on what the demand is for the skills. If you possess a skill that is in great demand, you can often dictate to the staffing service what your pay will be. If your skill is not in demand, you will find yourself at the mercy of whatever the service offers you.

Typically, services know exactly what type skills they are recruiting for. They know which client companies need managers, administrators, writers, trainers, lawyers, accountants, or engineers. Services know exactly how much they can bill per hour for these services, and from that bill rate they will figure out how much they can pay you, the temp, and still make their profit. So the temp often has to be very flexible to get work.

Being flexible means being realistic about how much you can expect per hour as a temp. Each temporary job can pay a different hourly salary. For example, you will earn less as an assistant to the vice president than you will as an architect or systems analyst. You may be paid different hourly wages depending on whether the service has a contract governing what they can bill for their temps at various businesses.

Joe G. was a project engineer in Philadelphia who worked for a company that developed and sold houses. He was making $65,000 a year when the company he worked for went bankrupt. Suddenly, Joe G. found himself without a job. He did not want to relocate, even though the demand for new homes had decreased dramatically where he lived.

Joe G. could not find a job in the housing industry where his expertise was. No one was hiring engineers who worked as project managers in developing new homes. He needed an income while he continued to look for a job, so he decided to temp.

Joe G. had always liked computers, had one at home, and had trained himself on several programs. He went to a staffing service and completed the application, indicating that he had experience as a computer consultant for software for small businesses. He learned through temping what worked well in computers for many small companies and was able to use his experience as a temp to make additional money.

Minimum Wage and Overtime

FEDERAL LAW PROVIDES UNDER THE FAIR LABOR STANDARDS ACT (FLSA) that every eligible employee must be paid a minimum wage and overtime pay as applicable. These wage and hour laws apply to staffing services as employers and are enforced through private lawsuits as well as by the Wage and Hour Division of the United States Department of Labor. Major cities across the nation have local Wage and Hour offices of the Labor Department; their addresses and telephone numbers are listed with the United States Government listings in the telephone directories. Since September 1, 1997, the basic minimum wage has been $5.15 an hour, whereas overtime pay is a rate of not less than one and one-half times your regular rate of pay. In other words, if you are paid the minimum wage of $5.15 an hour as your regular pay, then your overtime rate of pay would be $7.73 an hour. If your regular pay is $30 an hour, then your overtime rate of pay would be $45 an hour. Congress is considering amending the overtime pay law to allow employers to provide compensatory time off instead of paying overtime rates. For most professional executive and technical employees, minimum wage will not be an issue, but the subject of overtime pay may come up frequently.

You are entitled to overtime pay for all hours during a workweek that you are required to work in excess of 40 hours per week (unless your employment is exempted from minimum wage and overtime coverage), but you are not entitled by law to time off for holidays like Christmas and Thanksgiving and are not entitled to overtime pay for working holidays unless the hours worked total more than 40 hours for the week.

While federal minimum wage and overtime law (Fair Labor Standards Act or FLSA) does set basic minimum wage and overtime pay standards, there are a number of employment practices that the FLSA does not regulate. For example, the FLSA does *not* require:

1. Vacation, holiday, severance, or sick pay.

2. Meal or rest periods, holidays off, or vacations.

3. Premium pay for weekend or holiday work.

4. Pay raises or fringe benefits.

5. A discharge notice, reason for discharge, or immediate payment of final wages to terminated employees.

The FLSA does not provide wage payment or collection procedures for an employee's usual or promised wages or commissions in excess of those required by the FLSA. However, some states do have laws under which such claims (sometimes including fringe benefits) may be filed. The FLSA does not limit the number of hours in a day or days in a week an employee may be required or scheduled to work, including overtime hours, if the employee is at least 16 years old.

Who Is Entitled to Minimum Wage and Overtime?

GENERALLY, THE FEDERAL MINIMUM WAGE AND OVERTIME LAWS COVER any employee of a business that has workers engaged in interstate commerce; any employee of a business that produces or manufactures goods that are then shipped, sold, or distributed in interstate commerce; and any employee of a business that handles, sells, or otherwise deals in goods that have moved in interstate commerce. Almost every staffing service of any appreciable size would be engaged in interstate commerce.

Some categories of employees are exempt from minimum wage and overtime, however. Generally, exempt employees are executive, administrative, and professional employees, as well as outside sales employees, employees in certain computer-related occupations, employees of seasonal recreational businesses, and employees of small newspapers. But very few professional temps working through staffing services will meet the regulatory definition of "executive, administrative, or professional." In other words, most professional technical temps will be entitled to overtime pay when they work more than 40 hours in a workweek. Why?

The Department of Labor's definition of "executive, administrative, or professional" for purposes of the minimum wage and overtime law requires certain legal tests to be met. For example, to be exempt as an executive, administrative, or professional employee, the person must be considered a "salaried" employee who is paid full salary every workweek without regard to the number of days or number of hours actually worked. Further, the Department of Labor requires that executive, administrative, and professional exemptions claimed by employers must involve employees who direct or supervise the work of two or more full-time employees, who have the authority to hire and fire on behalf of the employer, who usually have

41

the authority to exercise a high level of independent judgment in their work, and who are not required to devote more than 20% of their time to nonmanagement, nonprofessional work. The issues as to whether a particular job is covered by or exempt from overtime pay requirements are complex. As a professional technical temp, if you believe you are entitled to overtime pay and are not receiving such additional compensation, then you should consult with the staffing service about it and with a lawyer or the Department of Labor's Wage and Hour Division, if necessary.

Generally, any employee who is eligible for minimum wage is also entitled to overtime pay; the few exemptions from overtime pay include such workers as commissioned employees of retail establishments; auto, truck, and aircraft sales workers; railroad and air carrier employees; certain media and broadcast business employees; and employees of motion picture theaters. Also, some industries are authorized by law to be partially exempt from overtime pay, such as hospital and healthcare establishments that agree with their employees to organize a 14-day workweek instead of the usual 7-day workweek, as well as partial exemptions for training and study purposes for some employees.

The area where most violations occur usually involves the number of hours worked. For example, David was placed through a staffing service to work as a paralegal in the corporate legal department of an Illinois textile manufacturing company that produced goods for sale across the nation. David was paid $20 per hour and worked Monday through Friday from 8:00 A.M. to 5:00 P.M., with one hour off for lunch. Often, he was required to sit in on late-afternoon meetings and found himself unable to leave until the meeting adjourned, which was seldom before 6:00 P.M. In addition, every other Saturday morning David was asked to come to a sales meeting where cross-training techniques were discussed by company supervisors, and occasionally he was required to attend company meetings in the evening where insurance and other benefit programs were explained. Usually, under the federal minimum wage and overtime laws, all of this time must be compensated: An eligible employee must be paid for all hours worked in a workweek, and in general, "hours worked" includes all time an employee is required to be on duty on the employer's premises or at any other prescribed place of work. Also included is any additional time the employee is allowed (i.e., suffered or permitted) to work by the employer.

Computing Overtime Pay

OVERTIME MUST BE COMPENSATED AT A RATE OF AT LEAST ONE AND one-half times the employee's regular rate of pay for each hour worked in a workweek in excess of the maximum allowable in a given type of employment. Generally, the regular rate includes all payments made by the employer to or on behalf of the employee (except for certain statutory exclusions). The following examples are based on a maximum 40-hour workweek.

Hourly Rate

If more than 40 hours are worked by an employee paid by the hour, at least one and one-half times the regular rate for each hour over 40 is due. *Example:* An employee paid $20 an hour works 44 hours in a workweek. The employee is entitled to at least one and one-half times $20 (i.e., at least $30) for each hour over 40. Pay for the week would be $800 for the first 40 hours, plus $120 for the four hours of overtime—a total of $920.

Salary

The regular rate for an employee paid a salary for a regular or specified number of hours a week is obtained by dividing the salary by the number of hours for which the salary is intended to compensate.

If, under the employment agreement, a salary sufficient to meet the minimum wage requirement in every workweek is paid as straight time for whatever number of hours are worked in a workweek, the regular rate is obtained by dividing the salary by the number of hours worked each week. To illustrate, suppose an employee's hours of work vary each week, and the agreement with the employer is that the employee will be paid $1000 a week for whatever number of hours of work are required. Under this agreement, the regular rate will vary in overtime weeks. If the employee works 50 hours in the week, the regular rate is $20 ($1000 divided by 50 hours). In addition to the salary, one and one-half the regular rate, or $30 is due for each of the 10 overtime hours, for a total of $1300 for the week. If the employee works 60 hours, the regular rate is $16.67 ($1000 divided by 60 hours). In that case, an additional $25 is due for each of the 20 overtime hours, for a total of $1500 for the week.

If a salary is paid on other than a weekly basis, the weekly pay must be determined in order to compute the regular rate and overtime pay. If the salary is for a half month, it must be multiplied by 24 and the product divided by 52 weeks to get the weekly equivalent. A monthly salary should be multiplied by 12 and the product divided by 52.

Other Labor Laws

IN ADDITION TO THE FEDERAL MINIMUM WAGE AND OVERTIME LAW, the Department of Labor administers a number of other labor laws that apply to the professional, executive, and technical temp worker. Among these are:

1. The Family and Medical Leave Act, which entitles eligible employees of covered employers to take up to 12 weeks of unpaid job-protected leave each year, with maintenance of group health insurance, for the birth and care of a child; for the placement of a child for adoption or foster care; for the care of a child, spouse, or parent with a serious health condition; or for the employee's serious health condition.

2. The Employee Polygraph Protection Act, which prohibits most private employers from using any type of lie detector test either for preemployment screening of job applicants or for testing current employees during the course of employment.

3. The Wage Garnishment Law, which limits the amount of an indi-

vidual's income that may be legally garnished and prohibits firing an employee whose pay is garnished for payment of a single debt.

4. The Immigration and Nationality Act, as amended, which requires employers to verify the employment eligibility of all individuals hired and keep Immigration and Naturalization Service forms (I-9) on file for at least three years and for one year after an employee is terminated; under the D-1 provisions, provides for the enforcement of employment conditions attested to by employers seeking to employ alien crew members to perform specified longshoring activity at U.S. ports; under the F-1 provisions, provides for the enforcement of attestations by employers seeking to use aliens admitted as students in off-campus work; under the H-1A provisions, provides for the enforcement of employment conditions attested to by employers of H-1A temporary alien nonimmigrant registered nurses; and under the H-1B provisions, provides for the enforcement of labor condition applications filed by employers wishing to employ aliens in specialty occupations and as fashion models of distinguished merit and ability.

Equal Pay Provisions

THE EQUAL PAY PROVISIONS OF THE FEDERAL MINIMUM WAGE AND overtime law prohibit sex-based wage differentials between men and women employed in the same establishment who perform jobs that require equal skill, effort, and responsibility and which are performed under similar working conditions. These provisions, as well as other statutes prohibiting discrimination in employment, are enforced by the Equal Employment Opportunity Commission. More detailed information is available from its offices, which are listed in most telephone directories under U.S. Government.

CHAPTER FOUR

Computer/Information Technology Jobs

IN THE AREA OF INFORMATION TECHNOLOGY, TEMPING IS ALL ABOUT supply and demand. If you can supply the computer skills that are demanded by businesses, you are in a profession that staffing services are aggressively recruiting for.

Staffing services want you, the expert in information technology, to join them. They are now offering great benefits and will pay you a salary, sometimes even when you are not out on a project. When you are not out on a job, many staffing services will help you get the training to stay ahead for future demands. That way, you will continue to work for them and consequently make money for them.

Flexibility is often a major requirement of temps with computer skills because of the frequent changes in this field. People who are systems analysts or programmers are constantly training themselves to keep up with innovations. There are staffing services that keep a pool of up-to-date trained people for special projects.

It is difficult to even attempt to address salaries for the professional technical temp who has specialized computer skills, because the types of skills are changing daily to meet the demands for information technology. Skills that are listed as hot today may be even hotter tomorrow and then may be obsolete next week. As a professional technical temp working in computer technology, your salary will constantly change, depending on whether businesses and, in return, staffing services are recruiting people with the skills and knowledge you possess.

Companies often call staffing services to provide temps in the computer field instead of hiring someone on their own, because many of the computer jobs are project work that will be completed in a span of six months to two years.

People who have computer skills that are in demand often work for a staffing service and move from job to job. These jobs may require mobility on the part of the temps. They are placed in positions that pay well. The staffing service often provides benefits to these highly skilled computer people to keep them employed by the service. Staffing services who place these temps often make a great deal of money because the skills are in such demand. Professional temps in these and other jobs may make more than people who are in the same jobs on a permanent basis. Because the temps may not be receiving benefits such as insurance, the extra money allows the temps to pay for the benefits on their own.

Pay in the area of information technology depends on experience with systems and applications. Salary for a senior programmer position depends on background and experience. Some staffing services work long-term—a year or longer. Know the salary that corresponds to your experience. Someone just graduating from college is entry-level. More experience pays more. Project management pays more. Those who have been in the market longer can command a higher salary. Many services prefer experienced people, as they cannot charge a fee for an entry-level worker. However, you can gain experience as a professional technical temp and you also have a chance of landing a full-time job working through a staffing service in a temp-to-hire situation.

Several staffing services provide representation in this area, for example, Robert Half International (RHI), Consulting Information Technology Staffing, General Employment Enterprises, and New Technology Services (NT).

There are various hiring methods for information technology people. The traditional way is where a staffing service hires a professional technical temp and pays the temp by the hour for hours worked. Those who are consultants usually work for a company like Arthur Andersen, which employs consultants who are hired by various businesses to come in and consult. There is a difference between what staffing services do and what Arthur Andersen does. If you do not believe this, just ask someone from Arthur Andersen!

Global Dynamics is a staffing service in California for those in the field of information technology. They place more than 70% of their temps, or consultants, as they are called by this company, in straight contract positions. That means someone is placed on a job, stays on it from start to finish, and then goes to another job, much like a traditional temporary worker.

Global Dynamics hires professional technical persons to temp for them by using a search list the company has developed. Those on this list have signed up with the company by using the Internet, by faxing their resumes, and many times by referrals from others.

People who temp for this information technology company have to complete a qualifying questionnaire and state whether they prefer to work on contract positions or on temp-to-hire positions. (Remember, a temp-to-hire job is a position you, the professional technical temp, try out for a period of weeks or months to give you and the company where you are temping ample time to determine if you are a match for each other.) Candidates must also list their required salary, their flexibility on relocation, and whether or not they are an independent contractor.

Global will then ask the candidate to complete a second questionnaire listing specific software skills. The client where the temp will be working may also review the questionnaire and the candidate's skills and resume before interviewing the candidate on the phone.

Many contract workers will then be interviewed in person. If that requires travel, most information technology temps will be expected to pay their own travel expenses as part of being a contract worker. The information technology temp can also expect to sign a release to submit to a background check and to take a drug test.

Paul Sharps, who is with Global Dynamics, says his business relies on word of mouth or referrals. Global pays a bonus to people who are currently working for Global who advise other skilled people to sign up with Global.

Another way information technology companies like Global find professional technical temps is by resumes. Sharps advises anyone sending a resume to Global to arrange the resume so that it is "keyword-driven."

Information technology companies that place the professional technical temp receive a great number of resumes. Sharps says most of these resumes are scanned by a computer that is programmed to look for certain key words, hence the term "keyword-driven." The scanner will seek key words and will also conduct a screen text search. Scanning resumes by computer enables companies like Global to develop a big database of professional technical workers.

Recruiters, those who place people on professional technical jobs, will go through the database and try to match skills to the jobs they are trying to fill. Sharps says candidates have a better chance of being placed if the resumes first list the experience skill, the job title, and then educational background. The experience skill list should include all the software and technical skills the person has. Those skills are what the recruiter will try to match to job openings. Firms like Global prefer that the resume have a technical summary at the beginning of the resume. For examples of how to do a keyword-driven resume, see the staffing services listed in the Appendix with Internet sites.

Information technology temps should review what is available on the Internet. When they find a company that can place their skills they can respond to many by e-mail. The text format offered by many companies through their Web site is a helpful tool for the information technology temp.

When sending a resume, always make sure it is a clean copy so that the scanner can easily review it. If the resume is faxed, the small print may not be read easily by the scanner. Sharps also says when someone submits a resume to Global it is helpful to include a good chronological list of the work accomplished. It is also helpful to list what is unique in the way the person did the work and what his or her role was in accomplishing the project.

Fred Sussman is the president of Technology Resource, a staffing service located in St. Louis, Missouri, which places people in information technology jobs. Sussman says there are three reasons businesses turn to services like Technology Resource who hire professional technical staffers. The first is the least-used reason, according to Sussman: that is, the business needs expertise that the business does not have. Sussman says that is when people like Arthur Andersen are called in to do high-level, high-profile consulting jobs.

The second reason outsiders are hired, according to Sussman, is that management does not want to take responsibility for unpleasant decisions that a business is going to make. Enter the consultants, who recommend measures such as downsizing, restructuring, and outsourcing—things that management knows it is going to have to do that will be unpopular with the rank-and-file employee.

The third reason management turns to outsiders is the reason there is such a need for those who have information technology skills, according to Sussman. Businesses need staff with skills. They need people to do short- and long-term projects. So, companies like Technology Resource have grown because they are constantly recruiting people with information technology skills for both short- and long-term jobs. Sussman says Technology Resource likes to recruit people by saying the company can help them "change jobs by changing assignments, not by changing employers."

How does Technology Resource do this? The company offers their workers two types of jobs. The first type is work that is project-oriented. The staffers are part of a team that is assigned a project and works on it from start to finish.

For example, Computer Company calls Technology Resource and requests a team of people to set up their help desk. Computer Company has just developed a new package of computer software that it has sold to a chain of office supply stores. The company expects calls about its system from new clients and does not want to hire a lot of full-time people to set up the help desk area.

Enter a team of experts from a staffing service like Technology Resource. This team is set up to develop a demonstration model of how the help desk will be run. The project could last several months, at the end of which this team that set up the help desk will go work together at another company through Technology Resource.

The second kind of assignment is working on a selective outsourcing job. When a company needs a particular type of work done on an ongoing basis it may hire a third party to do the work. For example, Company X needs to have a certain type of skill, so they call Technology Resource to find the skill for them. Technology Resource recruits people with the appropriate information technology skill and does the work for Company X. That means Technology Resource could do the work for several years. Company X saves money by not having the head count or payroll and benefits coming out of their budget. It is a win for companies like Technology Resource, because they can provide jobs for highly skilled people.

How do companies like Technology Resource and other information technology staffing services recruit their consultants or professional technical temps? They recruit through the Internet, through advertising, and especially through referrals. They look for people with skills to staff help desks, and others who have marketable information technology skills.

Technology Resource, like other information technology companies, qualifies employees by resumes, telephone interviews, and personal interviews. Sussman says his experience has taught him that it is 60–70% attitude and 30–40% technical skills that determine whether someone is the right fit for a particular professional technical job.

The professional technical information technology temp can expect to be measured for skills by taking software tests and by answering questions that will determine if the temp has the knowledge for certain jobs. Many services will ask for consent to perform background checks and will ask that you take a drug test. The information technology professional technical temp can also expect to have references checked and to sign confidentiality agreements. These agreements mean that the client who is paying the staffing service to provide information technology skills owns the work that the professional technical temp performs for the company. How does the information technology professional temp determine what salary to ask for? In this field it depends on supply and demand in the industry. Every 90 days there are new skills being developed and new demands for these skills. The salaries in this field change according to supply and demand.

To be a successful professional technical information technology temp, one should understand programming language tools, have good communications skills, understand database design, and have a grasp of business.

Training for the Computer/Information Technology Temp

THERE ARE TWO CURRENT SCHOOLS OF THOUGHT REGARDING TRAIN-ing for the information technology temp. Some firms do not want to spend time training the information technology person for the job. Many assignments that are temporary in nature require the person doing the job to hit the ground running. In other words, a company needs a job done right away and wants to hire someone for a limited time to do that job. That means the person needs the computer knowledge to do the existing job and does not have the time or luxury for any on-the-job training.

For example, Computer Company calls Anyone's Staffing Service for a computer programmer to install a certain type of system. The system needs to be up and running in 10 days. Anyone's Staffing must find a person who can start the first day with the knowledge to do the job. The service will not be able to fill the job with someone who has to learn how to do the job. That is not what Computer Company needs, and if Anyone's Staffing sends someone in who is not qualified to do the job, the service risks the assignment's not being performed to the satisfaction of Computer Company. Then Computer Company can ask for a refund of the money they paid to Anyone's Staffing, which will not be good for the reputation—or balance sheet—of Anyone's. Much of the work Anyone's Staffing obtains is by reputation, and if word gets out that Anyone's is not conducting business in a professional way, the service will risk loss of market share and going out of business.

The other school of thought for training is that information technology technical staffing services can teach professional technical temps new skills during times when they are not working for clients. Manpower Inc. has been doing this for several years through CBT Systems. Temps can learn different languages and skills in computer software at their own pace when not actually working. Technology Resource pays its employees an annual salary, and the company teaches them the latest technology when they are not out working.

Only you can decide what type of training you want as a professional technical temp. You will need to stay up-to-date regarding the skills demanded or sought by businesses in order to work effectively. You may want to consider working for a staffing service that has the foresight to train you so that your skills will stay current.

Computer programmers are one of the fastest growing groups for staffing services. That is because programmers write and maintain the detailed instructions—called programs or software—that give commands to a computer so that it is told what it must do.

Programmers may follow descriptions prepared by systems analysts. These analysts have carefully studied the task that the computer system is going to perform. These descriptions list the input required, the steps the computer must follow to process data, and the desired arrangement of the output. Some organizations, particularly smaller ones, do not employ systems analysts. Instead, workers called programmer-analysts are responsible for both systems analysis and programming.

What all of this means to the professional technical temporary is that there is a demand by smaller businesses for the skills of programmer-analysts. If you have the skills to work on both systems analysis and programming, a staffing service may recruit you to go work at smaller businesses that cannot afford to keep a full-time programmer-analyst on staff. As a professional technical temporary with these skills, you may be paid by a staffing service to become a full-time employee and be sent from small business to small business, where you will analyze and program different systems for small businesses.

Programmers, systems analysts, and programmer-analysts are being heavily recruited by staffing services because they have skills that are in demand. Many organizations do not employ any of these three types of information technology people; they depend on consultants and the staffing industry to send in individuals or teams of experts to help them with their information technology needs and to solve their problems. Information technology is changing so fast that it is often more cost-effective to outsource this function to staffing services than for a company to try to hire and keep a staff of experts trained in-house to meet its needs.

Programmers in software development who elect to work for a staffing service may be assigned to a team of experts from various fields to create software—either programs designed for specific clients or packaged software for general use—ranging from games and educational software to programs for desktop publishing, financial planning, and spreadsheets. Much of the programming being done today is the preparation of packaged software, one of the most rapidly growing segments of the computer industry. But despite the prevalence of packaged software, many programmers who become professional technical temps may be sent out on jobs that involve updating, repairing, and modifying codes for existing programs.

The professional technical temp who is a programmer is also in demand by staffing services for another important reason—debugging skill. When a program is ready to be tested, programmers run it to ensure that the instructions are correct and will produce the desired information. They prepare sample data that test every part of the program and, after trial runs, review the results to see if any errors were made. If errors do occur, the programmer must make the appropriate changes and recheck the program until it produces the correct results. This is called debugging the program. Therefore, many staffing services are looking for programmers who can debug or check a program for mistakes. More and more software programs are being developed, so there is a need for experienced programmers with this skill.

Finally, programmers working in a mainframe environment prepare instructions for the computer operator who will run the program. They may also contribute to a user's manual for the program. That means the programmer who is a professional technical temp can go in and work on a project that involves writing instructions for various operator's manuals. Once again, for the professional technical temp, it all goes back to supply and demand. For the programmer, that means developing very specific skills in programming so that the programmer's skills are always in demand or needed. The more in demand the skills are, the more the programmer can make as a professional technical temp or consultant.

Programs vary depending on the type of information to be accessed or generated. Some instructions for programming in the field of information technology are very simple. Others are complex. If several programmers work together as a team under a senior programmer's supervision, the person supervising should be paid more. The professional technical temp who is a senior programmer can expect to make more money than those he or she supervises.

Both applications and systems programmers can work today as professional technical temporaries or consultants. Applications programmers who become professional technical temps may work in business, engineering, or science. They can use their technical skills as temps to write software or to handle specific jobs, such as a program used in an inventory control system. They also may work alone or as part of a team of other professional technical temporaries and revise existing packaged software.

Systems programmers often maintain the software that controls the operation of an entire computer system. As a professional technical temp, a systems programmer could program or develop commands for terminals, printers, and disk drives. Because of their knowledge of the entire computer system, systems programmers who become professional technical temps may help other professional technical temps who are applications programmers determine the sources of problems that may occur with their programs. Therefore, both systems and applications programmers are often part of a team of experts when they work as professional technical temps.

Those in the information technology profession who work as professional technical temps can expect to work in a variety of businesses including, but certainly not limited to, data processing service organizations, firms that write and sell software, firms that provide engineering and management services, manufacturers of computer and office equipment, financial institutions, insurance carriers, educational institutions, and government agencies. The professional technical temp who is an applications programmer may work for all types of firms, whereas systems programmers who are temps will work for organizations with large computer centers or for firms that manufacture computers or develop software. The way technology is evolving will certainly change where these types of professional technical temps work. They may be able to choose to work from a home office that will allow them to use their skills through a network set up from home. The Watson Wyatt International consulting firm recently concluded in a survey that 51% of large information technology and telecommunications corporations allow their employees to telecommute today and 90% anticipate such telecommuting work policies within the next three years.

A growing number of programmers are employed on a temporary or contract basis. Rather than hiring programmers as permanent employees and then laying them off after a job is completed, employers increasingly are contracting with staffing services. A marketing firm, for example, may require the services of several programmers only to write and debug the software necessary to get a new database management system running. Such jobs may last from several months to a year or longer.

There are no universal training requirements for programmers, because employers' needs are so varied. Computer applications have become so widespread that computer programming is taught at most public and private vocational schools, community and junior colleges, and universities. However, the level of education and quality of training that employers seek have been rising due to the growth in the number of qualified applicants and the increasing complexity of programming tasks.

What does this mean to the professional technical temp? Many staffing services have their own testing and training programs. In fact, many staffing services call the professional technical temp a consultant so that this skilled person will have a better image. More and more staffing services are offering to pay these consultants or professional technical temps an annual salary rather than by the hour or by the project, so that the professional technical temp with these skills will work exclusively for their staffing service rather than go earn money for another service.

How does this pertain to training for the professional technical temp? It means that when the professional technical temp who is skilled in areas of information technology is not working, the staffing service will send the consultant or temp to a training facility. The professional technical temp, or consultant, stays on the payroll of the staffing service. That means that you, the professional technical temp, can continue to earn a salary from the staffing service and at the same time learn the latest skills that are in demand by businesses. The service who supplies the most temps with the skills most in demand wins!

The training of those in the profession of information technology is a critically important issue. The Institute for Certification of Computing Professionals (2200 East Devon Avenue, Suite 268, Des Plaines, IL 60018) confers the designation Certified Computing Professional (CCP) to those who have at least four years of experience or two years of experience and a college degree. To qualify, individuals must pass a core examination plus exams in two specialty areas, or an exam in one specialty area and two computing languages. Those with less experience may be tested for certification as an Associate Computer Professional (ACP). Certification is not mandatory, but it may give a job seeker a competitive advantage with staffing services.

More and more people will continue to use computers in their place of work and in their homes. So, companies want to hire people who can demonstrate new and different ways to use computers and the software that goes in the computer. There will continue to be a demand for programmers who can figure out how to put different types of software to work. If you can do that, you can make a lot of money as a professional technical temp.

Another opportunity for the professional technical temp who works in information technology is through networking computers so they can communicate with each other. This area will grow because many companies will merge and become global and want to communicate quickly. What better way than through networks that are linked?

The number and quality of applicants for programmer jobs have increased, so employers have become more selective. Graduates of two-year programs in data processing and people with less than a two-year degree or its equivalent in work experience are facing especially strong competition for programming jobs. Getting experience as a temp while attending college is a good way to be more placeable in the job market after completing your education.

Competition for entry-level positions by recent college graduates or technical school graduates will provide an opportunity for the professional technical temp, because temping is an excellent way for the recent graduate to gain experience. In fact, if you are an information technology student and have no work experience in your profession, why not sign up with a staffing service now and work part-time to gain experience? Take the example of Nancy, a senior in college. Nancy was within months of graduation with a degree in computer science. She had no work experience. As she attended career days at her college, she was interviewed by several companies for jobs, but the jobs she wanted always went to those with experience. Finally, Nancy caught on.

She signed up with a staffing service and started working four hours a night as a professional technical temp on a job where she tested computer software games. She worked part-time right up through graduation. The staffing service told her the business where she was working as a professional technical temp wanted to put her on a temp-to-hire job. The business and Nancy agreed to try each other out for a period of three months. At the end of the three months Nancy decided she did not want a full-time job at that particular company. She was able to qualify for a job she had previously applied for and had failed to get because of her lack of experience. Thanks to her temp job, Nancy acquired the skills and work experience to get the job she really wanted.

Consider working part-time as a professional technical temp while completing your studies for a degree. Many staffing services will design jobs around your class schedule. These services may even offer you a full-time job as a professional technical temp complete with benefits after you graduate. These types of positions can offer worldwide travel, should that be the type of job you are looking for. Other jobs for the recent college graduate that a staffing service can offer are those that are temp-to-hire. That means a business will try you out and you can try the business out for a period of weeks or months until you both are sure this is (or is not) the job you want. Temping is an excellent way to gain experience in the job market—you can try out jobs while you are also attending school.

Salary Suggestions for the Computer/Information Technology Temp

ACCORDING TO THE MOST RECENT SURVEY OF THE BUREAU OF LABOR Statistics, median earnings of programmers who work full-time are about $38,400 a year. The middle 50% earned between about $30,000 and $49,200 a year. The lowest 10% earned less than $22,000, and the highest 10%, more than $60,600.

According to Robert Half International, Inc., one of the nation's largest staffing services, starting salaries in large establishments for 1994 ranged from $29,500 to $36,500 for programmers; $36,000 to $47,000 for programmer-analysts; and $44,000 to $54,000 for systems analysts. Starting salaries in small establishments ranged from $25,000 to $34,000 for programmers and from $30,000 to $40,000 for programmer-analysts.

Again, the pay for the professional technical temp who is skilled in information technology depends upon availability of those experts and the number of professional and technical jobs that need to be filled. If there is a demand for your skills, you can command a higher salary than if there is no request for your skills. As previously mentioned in Chapter 3, one can factor an hourly salary based on an annual salary (refer to Figure 3.1 on page 35). Some staffing services may pay you more than the average annual salary of those in information technology and offer you no benefits in the belief that by receiving more pay, you can pick up the cost of the benefits. Other services will pay you by the project. Still others will offer you an annual salary with benefits. Again, you have to decide what type of pay structure is most appealing to you.

CHAPTER FIVE

Accounting, Bookkeeping, and Finance

P ERHAPS NO AREA OTHER THAN INFORMATION TECHNOLOGY HAS offered so much opportunity for the executive temp as that of accounting and finance. As the global economy grows and changes so does the need for those who can respond to financial requirements of downsizing, mergers, and acquisitions.

Business is competitive, and decision makers want a quick response when they buy or sell various companies. They turn to financial people to summarize the status of companies and analyze financial reports so the decision makers will know which ones to invest in and which to merge with. Those who know how to set up books, prepare taxes, audit, and especially combine these skills with computer knowledge will be in the catbird seat or potentially be able to write their own ticket when it comes to being a successful professional temp.

Accountants, certified public accountants or CPAs, auditors, and bookkeepers are in constant demand for financial, tax, and accounting work. Chapter 6 addresses the rapidly growing need for accounting and finance skills in the healthcare industry where government reimbursement to the hospitals, health maintenance organizations (HMOs), managed care organizations (MCOs), and preferred provider organizations (PPOs) are dependent on accounting procedures and audits.

According to *Employment Review*, April 1997, the accounting and finance profession "will continue to be in high demand as tax codes grow more arcane" and as healthcare issues, environmental issues, and North American Free Trade Agreement (NAFTA) issues demand these types of professionals.

There are four major groups of occupations that fall into the accounting and finance profession: public accounting, management accounting, government accounting, and internal auditing. The good news for the professional technical temp is that all four areas use staffing services.

Public accountants are known for working on tax matters with companies and with individuals, which means they use staffing firms at the peak of tax season. Other public accountants work for corporations, individuals, and nonprofit organizations. Every aspect of public accounting uses staffing services.

Those in management accounting work in corporations or businesses and manage the financial information of the company that employs them. They are in the private as opposed to the public (government) sector. Management accountants use temps to help them find out information for the companies whose accounting they manage. This type of work includes working on budgets, asset management, cost, and performance.

Those who work in government accounting are accountants and auditors. Federal, state, and local agencies may use professional technical temps. The government sector and the private sector differ in that the government puts its staffing business out for bid. That means the government lists the type of jobs for which it needs a staffing service, and various services propose or bid for the projects. A government agency then selects a vendor from the bid process and awards its business to one or more staffing services. If you want to work in governmental accounting, you most likely will have to work through a staffing service that has been awarded a bid by the government. The professional technical financial temp who works for government can audit various agencies and help examine the records of those businesses that are regulated by the government, such as banks and financial institutions.

The fourth financial field where professional technical temps are used is internal auditing. If you temp for internal auditors, you will work on researching and checking business records to ensure that the business is being managed correctly.

Both public accounting firms and private companies are constantly searching for qualified accounting and finance temps for several reasons. First, the annual tax season, which begins in January or February each year and ends April 15 for most individuals, places ever-increasing demands on the capacity of the accountants. A successful public accounting firm must increase its professional staff each tax season, and near the end of each quarter for its corporate clients, to meet this demand. Second, as noted previously, the tremendous explosion in the delivery of healthcare services, consolidation of hospital ownership nationally, mergers of hospital management companies, and increasing government regulation of Medicaid, Medicare, and similar programs necessitates that the healthcare industry employ an ever-growing number of accountants. Since there is no direct contact between these accountants and the customer base, the use of accountant temps is facilitated. A third reason mandating the use of accountant temps is the traditional occurrence of illness, maternity leave, family crisis, unexpected resignation, fluctuating workload, and special project.

In their 1997 salary survey, Robert Half Accountemps, based in Menlo Park, California, reported an increase in pay rates for accountant temps ranging from 1.4% to 4%. Depending on the region of the country and level of experience and expertise, accountant temps are paid anywhere from $18–$20 an hour up to $35–$40 an hour. People who work as professional technical temps in the accounting field have several types of jobs from which to choose. The positions include a variety of financial skills. For example, someone in accounting can be classified in many different ways: full-charge bookkeeper; staff accountant; accounting supervisor; someone with cost accounting, tax, or healthcare experience; accounts receivable; accounts payable; and credit and collections.

Another area where staffing services place people in temporary and full-time jobs is in payroll. Companies call staffing services and ask for payroll specialists who have experience in automated or computerized payroll.

Staffing services that specialize in placing accountants code them according to skills and experience to determine what the pay will be.

Some staffing services include a salary survey for accounting and finance on their Web sites. A 1996–1997 survey by the Bureau of Labor Statistics says accountants with limited experience had a median income of $25,400, and the most experienced had median earnings of $57,200. Public accountants working for public accounting firms with limited experience had median earnings of $28,100, and experienced median income was $48,800. If you want to determine what your salary should be as a professional temp in the area of finance, you can compute the hourly salary by referring to the formula in Figure 3.1 on page 35.

The tax season demands an increase in the number of accountants and calls for a lot of accounting. Temps with tax experience may choose to work only during this time of the year. Andy was one such person. Andy started working for a public accounting firm when he graduated from college in 1955. He started out as a junior accountant, then became a staff accountant, rose to senior accountant, and retired as an accounting supervisor for the tax division of one of the Big Six accounting firms.

When Andy retired he found that he had more time on his hands than he wanted; he decided to go back to work two days a week during the tax season. Rather than freelance, he decided to let a staffing service find a part-time job for him. The service was glad to have Andy as an applicant, except for the fact that he did not have any computer skills.

The staffing service he chose decided to turn the situation into a win-win for both the service and Andy. On the days Andy was not working, he spent time in the staffing service's training area and learned Lotus and Excel. He had always had a fear of computers, and this helped him overcome his fear and impatience with computer software. As it turned out, Andy found that using a computer was not as difficult as he had thought it would be. He was able to work two days a week as a tax accountant. The other days, he volunteered at a job placement service helping those over 50 learn computer skills to make themselves more marketable.

People who are financial analysts are also having success in the world of professional technical temping. These include credit analysts and budget analysts as well as the general business analysts. They help set both short- and long-term budgets, as well as set short- and long-term projections for various projects.

There are now more advanced financially skilled people who are working temp, such as chief financial officers and controllers.

Staffing services look for computer skills for those in the finance and accounting world who want to work temp. In addition to the Internet, the software skills many services look for are Excel and Lotus as well as Solomon, Quickbooks, Peachtree, and Great Plans.

If you choose to work full-time as a professional technical temp in the financial field, consider investing in a laptop computer that has some kind of standard financial software on it. There is a demand for the professional technical temp who has combined accounting or auditing knowledge with computer programming skills, and can solve problems and help develop software that specifically meets financial recordkeeping and analysis requirements. These programs format or arrange various kinds of financial information that accountants and auditors are constantly compiling and explaining. As financial people continue to work with computers, they will design programs that are specific to the needs of public, management, and government accountants and auditors. That means if you are a person who can combine your financial skills with computer knowledge, you will not have any trouble selecting the type of jobs you want as a temporary professional technical worker or as someone who wants to temp your way into a full-time job.

If you do not have any computer skills or just want to increase your skills, many staffing services will work with you to accomplish this and train you. Most services will ask you what, if any, skills you have on the computer. Some services will even test your abilities on certain software. You may also be tested on accounting skills, such as your knowledge of debit and credit, and of 10-key (and maybe whether you have 10-key by touch or by sight, which means you must look at a keypad before entering the numbers into a system). Some staffing services have specific written questions that test whether you have the background you say you have as someone who has worked in accounting or finance.

If you want to learn a software program that will help you as an accountant or finance person while working as a temp, there are several ways to accomplish this. First, you can tell the service what skills you want to learn. The service may train you in-house, that is, on a computer in the office of the staffing service. Some of the staffing service programs are self-tutorial, so you can learn at your own pace. The service may charge you a nominal fee for teaching you the program. Many of the progressive or better staffing services will allow you to come in and work on their equipment and learn on the days they do not have work for you.

Another way to learn accounting software programs is on the job. A staffing service may send you out to work on an accounting assignment where you will be exposed to a software program you know nothing about. Most reputable services will tell the people you are working with you need time to learn the program and will factor in the amount of time you need to learn the software with the time for the assignment. For example, Lois signed up to be an accountant with a staffing service and was told there was a six-week job available where she would be working on Quattro Pro and Excel. She was proficient in Excel but had never learned Quattro Pro. She took the six-week job, and the staffing service told the company where she would be temping that she could do everything the job required except the Quattro Pro. The service adjusted the hourly bill rate for the client, which allowed Lois to learn the software. The client was satisfied, because Lois was billed at a lower rate while she was learning the software. Lois came away from the six-week job with more skills than she had before she started.

In an interview, Mark Nightingale, who is an area manager for Robert Half International (RHI) Accountemps, the largest staffing service for accountants, employing thousands of people each year as professional technical temps, said that the skills that are in demand by Accountemps are those that are in demand according to the current economy. Those needs can change. If you have the following skills your chances are high that you can be a successful temp, according to Nightingale: speadsheet, integrated accounting, up-to-date software packages such as Peachtree and Accpac, 10-key, bank reconciliation, general ledger, collections, and credit.

Most staffing services who place accounting and financial people operate in the same way. You submit a resume, and then you check or list all of the skills you have. If you check out various staffing services on the Internet, you will see there are hundreds of skills from which you can select. The staffing service will then match your skills to the needs of their clients. You will then be paid according to the skills you are using. Nightingale said Accountemps pays their employees a salary based on the skills sheet, and some people may earn less as a temp than they did as a full-time employee.

It is important to remember that in accounting and finance, like any other area of temping, you will be paid for the skills you are using the day(s) you are working. For example, Clark listed all the skills he had as an experienced chief financial officer (CFO) for a medium-sized company where he had earned an annual salary of $102,000. When his company was acquired and Clark's position was eliminated, Clark decided to do some professional temping. The staffing service he worked with offered him the highest-paying temporary assignment they had available at the time Clark wanted to work. The temp job called for someone with the skills of a manager who had experience at being an analyst for a medium-sized company. Therefore, Clark was paid an hourly salary based on the skills he would be using on that temporary job, which was a much lower hourly salary than he would have been paid had he been placed as a temp on a job calling for a CFO with all the skills he had used in his previous full-time job.

Nightingale said Accountemps often recruits employees from other temps. He said, "Good people know other good people." The company recruits from college campuses, and if you have a four-year degree you can work temp and gain work experience. That experience can help you work yourself into a full-time job. He went on to say that approximately 30% of temporary jobs filled by Accountemps become permanent jobs.

Robert Half Accountemps also recruits from professional and networking groups. When asked what the best characteristic is for a professional technical person who wants to have successful experience as a temp, Nightingale said, "A good attitude makes a winning temp."

Your salary as an accounting and finance temp will depend on supply and demand; in other words, what skills businesses requesting financial temps are looking for. If there are not a lot of people available with the skills that are being requested, those skilled people can expect to be paid well. If there are more people available than there are jobs open for certain skills, those people will be paid less.

Market surveys indicate that accountants with great experience who temp can expect to earn $37,000 to $83,000 on an annualized basis. Accountants with relatively little experience can expect to earn $26,500 to $40,000 on an annualized basis.

You may check or list what types of positions you are applying for, what geographic area you want to work in, and the software skills you have. After you complete a questionnaire for the staffing service, your application will be forwarded to an office where a representative will call you if you have the skills matching the positions the staffing service is trying to fill.

In Los Angeles, for example, many of the staffing services named earlier provide professional accountant temps. Similar services are offered in the New York area by Robert Half Accountemps, Accountants on Call (a division of Adecco), Access Accounting Professionals, Vanguard Accounting Temporaries, Peak Staffing Services, Account Pros, Temporary Accounting Professionals, and Accountants Overload. Accountemps is among the first and still the largest staffing service that specializes in accounting and other financial skills. Please refer to the Appendix for a list of staffing services that place temps with accounting and financial skills.

CHAPTER SIX

Healthcare and Science

H EALTHCARE TEMPS TRADITIONALLY INCLUDE NOT JUST HOSPI-
tal and nursing home employees, but also the people who staff
doctors' offices, clinics, and healthcare companies. The temp staff
can include anyone from the receptionist to the hospital administrator and from the physician's assistant to the doctor. Medical support
staff includes those who file insurance claims with Medicare and
those who do the credit and collections. Then there is the traditional
medical staff—the doctors or physicians, nurses, lab technicians,
physician's assistants, and nurse-practitioners.

In the next few years as hospital management companies and insurance companies exert more and more dominance over health
maintenance organizations (HMOs), preferred provider organizations (PPOs), and medical practice, an increasing number of doctors, registered nurses, licensed practical nurses, and physician's
assistants are expected to seek out staffing services to enhance their
employment. This means more opportunity for those in the medical
profession to earn a living as a professional temp or to use temping
as a means to find a full-time job in healthcare.

The present and future trend for medical practice and delivery of
healthcare services is to utilize the HMO and PPO concepts. The
central focus of these types of organizations is to provide quality
medical services while conserving and limiting the monetary costs.

Thus, HMOs are essentially groups of doctors, hospitals, and medical practitioners who have formed an organizational alliance to increase their financial power and to maximize their economies of scale.

Because an HMO represents a large number of healthcare
providers it can achieve reductions in costs, discounts, and other sav-

ings. Of course, HMOs usually mean more depersonalized medical services for the individual patient because of the HMO size and organizational complexity (especially as compared to a family doctor who has treated the same patients their entire lives). At an HMO you may see a different doctor on every visit.

Preferred provider organizations can result in a similar loss of individualized care when a health care plan requires an individual to use only a doctor or clinic of his or her PPO. Oftentimes this means patients will be treated by a doctor and/or nurse that they do not know.

What does this mean for the staffing industry? The greatest increase of the next generation of temps may very well be doctors, nurses, and backroom or nonoffice-support medical staff. Healthcare practitioners have the opportunity to move from one practice to another to another without hindrance, as the nature of these healthcare services is changing. Patients of HMOs and PPOs no longer expect to personally know their doctor or nurse, and therefore an entirely new employment market is in the process of being created.

There is a growing need for the traditional front office staff, which includes office support. Those technical and professional temps with a knowledge of healthcare claims for billing purposes will have a very good chance of finding temporary and permanent employment. The need for accountants and auditors is growing quickly in the healthcare industry. With new regulations from the government and a growing complexity in billing to patients and reimbursements to doctors and hospitals, a healthcare accountant and auditor are not a luxury but a necessity.

Matthew is one of the many people who are turning to the healthcare industry as a way to use their accounting skills. He earned his degree in accounting six years ago from a university and went to work for a state government agency. While Matthew was working for the state agency he studied for his CPA exam. He even passed three parts of the exam.

After six years, a new governor was elected on his promise to downsize and decrease the number of people on the government payroll in Matthew's state. One of the ways the governor did this was to merge several state agencies together to form a new department. Matthew had supported the new governor, and like many other state employees assumed his job was secure and went on about his daily business.

Imagine how stunned Matthew was one Friday afternoon when his supervisor called him in to tell him his position was being eliminated when the agencies merged. Matthew was given two weeks' severance pay and told to have a nice life. Matthew had no idea what to do next. There he was, in his early thirties. He only knew he wanted to avoid the same type of government position he had tried before.

When Matthew was employed by the state, he always listened to the radio on the way to work, and he remembered hearing commercials for staffing services that placed accountants on jobs. Matthew had never considered temping. He thought it was only for secretaries, not accountants. Matthew also knew he had nothing to lose and he needed immediate income.

So, Matthew signed up with several staffing services that specialized in placing accountants on jobs. Matthew accepted a six-month assignment at a hospital through one of the services. He was paid $14.58 an hour.

While temping there, Matthew received on-the-job training in the accounting procedures for Medicare reimbursement. There are a lot of tedious procedures to billing patients and making sure the doctors and hospitals are reimbursed by the government. Matthew was able to take the knowledge he gained in this temp position and upgrade his skills. He even used this time to pass the other part of the CPA exam so that he became a certified public accountant. The hospital told the staffing service Matthew was working for that they wanted to hire him. Matthew accepted the position and started out at an annual salary of $44,000.

Some hospitals choose to outsource entire functions to staffing services that provide professional temps. These services need experience in interviewing, employment law, recruiting, and benefits. Human resources managers, employee relations managers, and compensation analysts are being hired as temporary employees to do projects. That means personnel offices want to keep their numbers of employees lean and a core group.

Physicians sometimes delegate the management of their offices to staffing services. The skills needed to work as a professional technical temp in a doctor's office vary. Experience with the filing of insurance claims and Medicare reimbursement is in demand today. There is also a huge demand for those skilled in accounting or finance who know how the system works for Medicare reimbursement. If you do not have experience in this area and want to learn, take advantage of any temporary assignment that will give you on-the-job-training. Again, like anything else, it is a matter of supply and demand. There is a demand for those skilled in Medicare reimbursement and staffing services want to recruit people with these skills.

There are more and more traditional medical areas using temps, such as nurses, physical therapists, and even physician's assistants. Physician's assistants usually work with one physician, and because of this close relationship have been slow to start temping. As healthcare looks for a way to cut costs, this could change, and more people in clinics may be referred to physician's assistants and to nurse practitioners, whereas in the past these patients would have been referred to a doctor.

A physician may work temp in one hospital while the hospital recruits temporary doctors. There are companies that furnish medical temps nationwide.

Jack Maxwell, president of Maxwell Medical Staffing, is part of a business that places people who are physical therapists, occupational therapists, and speech therapists. His company has had to go outside the United States to fill U.S. jobs. The positions pay an average of $40,000 to $45,000 annual salary depending on education and experience. The temporary jobs pay $18 to $24 an hour depending on education and experience.

Maxwell recruits from New Zealand, Canada, Ireland, Scotland, England, Israel, South Africa, and Zimbabwe to create the supply to meet the demand. Maxwell has had great success because these staffers like to travel and gain experience. Some stay, and some return home.

More than half of Maxwell's medical placements go into a temporary assignment and turn it into a permanent position. This is a win-win outcome for the staffing company, because it gives Maxwell another success story and because the medical staffers who are placed refer others to Maxwell. Most people in the medical profession turn the temporary jobs into permanent ones because they have a good attitude and a can-do mentality, according to Maxwell. The staffers try to fit in and do a such a good job that the companies where they are temping want to create a position for them rather than lose them to another temporary job.

Many people who temp in the medical profession use the temp jobs as a way to broaden their skills and get more on-the-job training. Maxwell believes there will be more of a global market for those willing to work in the medical profession as temps, because of a global need for medical staffers—just like other white-collar professional technical temps—to go to other countries and work on short- and long-term projects. So, if you want to travel, join the ranks of the professional technical temp.

Marion was a graduate of a physical therapist program at an accredited university in England. She had always wanted to travel and work in America, and wanted to live and work in a small town as opposed to a large city.

Marion did some research on the Internet and completed a questionnaire with a medical staffing company. She then faxed her resume to the company. After the staffing company completed reference checks and background checks on Marion, she was offered a nine-month temporary assignment in a small town in Iowa. The staffing service also asked Marion to take a personality test so that the service could locate a job that would be suitable for her.

She completed the necessary legal forms to work in the United States. In other words, she provided a green card for her I-9 form, then flew to Iowa on a ticket provided by the staffing service and met with a representative of the service. The representative gave Marion a thorough indoctrination regarding the hospital where she would be working: dress code, work hours, where to eat, the types of personalities that worked well in the hospital, as well as the politics of the town where she would live. The staffing service also located several apartments to choose from, but Marion was responsible for paying her rent.

The staffing representative gave Marion her job description and helped her find transportation to her job. The staffing service paid for the fare, but once Marion was at the job she was on her own. She had a rough couple of first weeks. The staffing service told her about some of the people she would be working with and even shared who the service thought would be the most receptive to Marion, a foreigner, and who would not.

Small-town America was nice, but Marion found it took a little while for people to make friends with her. Some of the people the staffing service told her about took her out to dinner and invited her to join their reading club. After the first month she began receiving regular invitations for social events, even dates. She also learned to take the initiative for her social life and after two months felt more at home. When the end of her assignment came up, the hospital asked the staffing service if they could hire her.

Marion had to continue to supply the legal paperwork necessary to keep working in the United States. She decided to stay on another three months as a temp, then evaluate if she wanted to stay in Iowa or work on another temporary assignment elsewhere.

The staffing service told her that many rural hospitals needed her skill as a physical therapist, and they would also work with her on relocating to a larger city if she chose to. The great thing about temping is that it allows flexibility in making a decision about going permanent. Marion still had income and benefits as a professional temp and had her freedom too.

When hospital administrators lose their jobs as a result of consolidation, those professionals often go into the management and administration of rehab centers, surgery centers, radiology centers, and similar related areas. Hospital administrators may temp while the consolidation group selects a new manager.

When a foreign automotive parts company decided to open a plant that would supply automobile parts to a major car company, the company looked for a small town that had an industrial park with abundant geographic space to grow. The company selected a site in Texas and started building a plant that would provide 2000 jobs for the small town.

The administrator of the local hospital realized the hospital would need to expand its services in order to serve the additional growth the plant would bring to the community. The administrator was particularly concerned about the emergency room. The administrator called a professional staffing service that specialized in healthcare, and the service sent one of their representatives to meet with hospital management. They analyzed the situation and discussed the needs of the hospital.

The staffing service recommended that the service staff the emergency room and the physical therapy functions for the next two years. The next two years would determine the hospital's actual needs in the community. At the end of two years, as the plant opened, the hospital and staffing service would evaluate how effective the service had been in meeting the health care needs of the community.

The U.S. Department of Health and Human Services is reporting a 40% shortage of nurses in the country today. Healthcare is looking to staffing services to help with the demands of rural hospitals and rural medical practices. Some standards in rural areas may not be as high for some programs as in urban areas, so staffing services may be able to help rural clinics with candidates who cannot easily find jobs in urban areas.

In the New York area some medical temp staffing is done through Gregory & Gregory Medical Staffing. In New Orleans, Norrell Staffing Services; in Washington, DC, Olsten Health Services and Progressive Nursing Staffers, Inc.; and in Atlanta, Starmed Health Personnel, Inc. For a more detailed listing of staffing services who place temps in the medical profession, please refer to the Appendix or search the Internet for appropriate Web sites.

Doctors

JOB PROSPECTS ARE ESPECIALLY GOOD FOR PRIMARY CARE PHYSICIANS, such as family practitioners and internists, and for geriatric and preventive care specialists, according to the Bureau of Labor Statistics' 1996–1997 *Occupational Outlook Handbook.* Because of efforts to control healthcare costs and increased reliance on guidelines that often limit the use of specialty services, a lower percentage of medical specialists will be in demand. Thus, more recent medical school graduates may want to consider temping due to the changing structure in healthcare. Shortages are being reported in the specialty area of general surgery in some rural and low-income areas, because physicians find these areas unattractive due to low earnings potential, isolation from medical colleagues, or other reasons—not because of any overall shortage of surgeons. Such regional shortages create additional opportunities for temping.

What does this mean to the doctor who may want to temp? Unlike their predecessors, newly trained physicians face radically different choices of where and how to practice. Many new physicians are less likely to enter solo practice and more likely to take salaried jobs or temporary staffing positions in group medical practices, clinics, and HMOs in order to have regular work hours and the opportunity for peer consultation. Others will take salaried positions or temp positions simply because they cannot afford the high costs of establishing a private practice while paying off student loans.

How does the physician determine what his or her pay should be as a professional temp? Physicians have among the highest earnings of all occupations. According to the most recent Bureau of Labor Statistics survey, average (mean) income, after expenses, for allopathic physicians is about $189,000, and median income is $156,000. The middle 50% earn between $108,000 and $240,000.

Self-employed physicians—those who own or are part owners of their medical practices—have higher median incomes than salaried physicians. Earnings vary according to number of years in practice, geographic region, hours worked, skill, personality, and professional reputation. As shown in Figure 6.1, median income of allopathic physicians, after expenses, also varies by specialty.

Recent surveys show average salaries of medical residents range from $30,753 for those in their first year of residency to $41,895 for those in their eighth year, according to the Association of American Medical Colleges.

Physician's Assistants

ACCORDING TO A 1994 UNIVERSITY OF TEXAS SURVEY OF HOSPITALS and medical centers, the median annual salary of physician's assistants, based on a 40-hour week and excluding shift or area differentials, was $48,264. The average minimum salary was $37,639, and the average maximum was $57,005.

According to the American Academy of Physician Assistants, me-

FIGURE 6.1 Median Income of M.D.s after Expenses	
Medical Field	*Annual Income*
All physicians	$156,000
Radiology	$240,000
Surgery	$225,000
Anesthesiology	$220,000
Obstetrics/gynecology	$200,000
Pathology	$170,000
Emergency medicine	$164,000
Internal medicine	$150,000
Pediatrics	$120,000
Psychiatry	$120,000
General/Family practice	$110,000
Source: American Medical Association	

dian income for all physician's assistants in 1994 was $53,284; median income for first-year graduates was $44,176. Income varies by specialty, practice setting, geographical location, and years of experience. Refer to Figure 3.1 on page 35 in order to determine how to calculate your pay as a professional temporary physician's assistant.

Nurses

NURSES DO IT ALL. MANY PEOPLE WOULD RATHER TALK TO A NURSE than to a doctor. While state laws govern the tasks registered nurses may perform, it is usually the work setting that determines their day-to-day duties.

Hospital nurses form the largest group of nurses who work for staffing services. Another group consists of those who work in the office of a physician. Office nurses assist physicians in private practice, clinics, surgery centers, emergency medical centers, and health maintenance organizations (HMOs). They prepare patients for and assist with examinations, administer injections and medications, dress wounds and incisions, assist with minor surgery, and maintain records. Some also perform routine laboratory and office work.

There is opportunity for nurses who want to work as professional temps. Kelly Services and Olsten, two of the larger national staffing services, have developed divisions that work with health care professionals like nurses. There is a very competitive market, with staffing services competing for the skills of the competent nurse. But it also depends upon supply and demand.

For example, if you are a nurse and live in a city where several staffing services are advertising for your skills, you can probably work whenever you want to. On the other hand, if you live in an area where many nurses are being laid off, then there will not be as big a demand for your skills.

Nan was a registered nurse with experience in cardiac care. When she moved with her husband from one small town to a larger one, she decided to start a family and change her hours of work outside the home. Before her move, Nan had supervised the care of those who had heart surgery. She wanted to continue using her nursing skills, but did not want the responsibility of supervising others while her children were young.

The city where Nan moved had several staffing services that placed skilled nurses like herself on temporary assignments. Nan was able to find a job that allowed her to work the hours she wanted to as a nurse and earn competitive wages. The staffing service placed her in a variety of jobs, including hospitals, doctors' offices, and home healthcare.

Home health nurses can work as temps. Services set up nurses to go into people's homes and care for and instruct patients and their families. Home health nurses care for a broad range of patients, such as those recovering from illnesses and accidents, cancer, and childbirth. They must be able to work independently. The same can be said for nurses who work in nursing homes.

Public health nurses work in government and private agencies and in clinics, schools, retirement communities, and other community settings as temporary workers. Don't forget: As the generation of baby boomers ages, the demand for healthcare will increase for the parents of baby boomers, the children of baby boomers, and for baby boomers themselves. The more demand there is for skills in health care, the more people are needed who can provide healthcare, creating many different opportunities for the professional technical temp with healthcare skills.

Nurse-practitioners are also hired as temps, because they provide basic healthcare and in some states can prescribe medications. The professional technical temp who is a nurse-practitioner may work with other healthcare temps who are nurse-anesthetists and certified nurse-midwives. There will always be a need for traditional hospital nurses, but a large number of new nurses who are professional technical temps will be employed in home health, long-term, and ambulatory care.

Employment for temps in home health care is expected to grow quickly and staffing services will be recruiting nurses who want to use their professional skills to assist people with healthcare needs. More and more people will prefer to be cared for in their own home; therefore, staffing services will want to find the skills to meet these future demands.

Employment in nursing homes for temps is expected to grow much faster than average due to increases in the number of people in their eighties and nineties, many of whom will require long-term care. In addition, the financial pressure on hospitals to release patients as soon as possible should produce more nursing home admissions. This is another opportunity for the professional technical temp who has the skills needed to staff nursing homes.

The use of temps in units to provide specialized long-term rehabilitation for stroke and head injury patients or to care for and treat Alzheimer's victims will also increase steadily.

Current information available from the Department of Labor Bureau of Labor Statistics states median weekly earnings for the middle 50% of full-time salaried registered nurses are between $542 and $838. A University of Texas survey conducted in 1994 of hospitals found that the median annual salary for nurses based on a 40-hour week and excluding shift or area differentials was: head nurses—$50,700, clinical nurse specialists—$47,674, professional nurse-practitioners—$47,432, nurse-anesthetists—$37,444, and staff nurses—$35,256.

Scientists

THOSE WITH SCIENTIFIC SKILLS CAN ALSO FIND WORK THROUGH staffing services today. In a recent story on scientist temps, the *Washington Post* told how Kelly Services has staffed the Oak Ridge National Laboratory in Tennessee with temporary workers. Kelly Services has a niche some of the other national staffing services do not, because the Kelly Scientific Resources division places people who are scientists. The *Washington Post*'s January 20, 1997, article discussed a "new breed of Kelly temp: the scientist for hire." The Oak Ridge National Laboratory's use of temps is part of a growing trend of corporations and governments treating science as a business. Research and laboratory experiments are being outsourced to staffing services.

Businesses believe that hiring staffing services like Kelly Services will allow them to save money by letting someone else do the hiring and supervising of scientist temps.

Kelly Scientific Resources has 15 offices and is expected to open 10 more in the near future. In the *Washington Post* article, Rolf Kleiner, vice president of Kelly Scientific Resources, said, "We offer everything from low-level animal handler and glassware washer all the way up to the PhDs. They span the disciplines of chemistry, biochemistry, molecular biology, physics, geology, environmental science, you name it."

Manpower Inc. has joined with the American Institute of Physics to place physicist temps. The *Washington Post* said that On Assignment staffing service of Calabasas, California, is "the country's largest temp agency specializing only in scientists. On any given day, said chief executive officer H. Tom Buelter, more than 2500 On Assignment scientists are working across the country in more than 60 laboratories."

Some of the scientific skills searched for by various staffing services include research assistants, pharmaceutical technicians, pharmacists, biologists, biotechnologists, chemists, environmentalists, genetic engineers, laboratory assistants, and laboratory technicians.

The healthcare industry is closely tied to the scientific industry. Many of the jobs for scientists may also be advertised and recruited for by staffing services that recruit for healthcare providers. For example, pharmacists are hired by some companies that also recruit and hire nurses and lab technicians. People who have clinical trials experience have opportunities in the staffing industry, because so much of their work is likely to be project-oriented. For example, if a company is trying to discover whether a certain type of drug is available, the company will call a staffing service like Maxwell Clinical Trials Support Services to send out professional technical temps to research what drugs are available relating to a certain topic.

CHAPTER SEVEN

Engineers

E NGINEERING IS A PROFESSION THAT HAS NOT ENJOYED GREAT use of temporary staffing services in the past, but that situation has quickly changed in recent years. Now, due to a shortage of engineers in almost every region of the country, employers and recruiters are seeking specialists in nearly all areas of engineering and architecture, according to the *National Business Employment Weekly* for March 23–29, 1997. That report, by managing editor Perri Capell, concludes that larger engineering firms are "adding staff only to meet specific surgical-type needs so they won't have to lay off employees if business slows." Because of this change in dynamic, more and more professional staffing services are concentrating on the engineering profession.

It is just after 9:00 A.M. and Martin and other members of the development group are meeting to discuss a prototype for a new fast-food restaurant. Martin has been working on this project for two months and expects to complete his part of the work in a few more weeks. When this project ends, Martin will not only move on to a new project, he will be working for a new company. Martin is one of the growing number of engineers to join the ranks of temporary professional employees.

Martin, a civil engineer, had worked for a large regional grocery store chain headquartered in the Midwest. Martin's job involved evaluating sites for new stores and modifying the chain's standard store plan for local site conditions and building codes. With 10 years of experience and great performance reviews, he had felt pretty secure about his future. But that was before his company was acquired by one of its competitors. Instead of a job, Martin suddenly found himself with a severance package that included a few months of salary continuation and an appointment with an outplacement firm.

The outplacement firm hired by the acquiring company suggested Martin update his computer skills so that he would be more marketable. They also suggested he sign up with several staffing services to find temporary or temp-to-hire jobs. Martin was a little reluctant to go down this path at first because he thought it might hurt his chances of finding another full-time permanent job. This reluctance was overcome by the realization that his severance package would soon run out. He talked to friends, the outplacement firm, and even an adviser at the technical school where he was taking his computer classes to get information on staffing services representing the engineering disciplines. He ended up with a list of three companies that specialized in placing engineers. Two of the companies were national companies without a local office. Martin was able to send them his resume and application via the Internet.

Through one of the national staffing services Martin was offered a choice of jobs. The first was project work, which meant he would be paid a specific amount each month for a few months until the project was completed. This particular project was in his hometown and would require very little travel. However, it was a short-term assignment and provided no benefits. His other option was to join the staffing service as a consultant, or full-time temporary employee. The staffing service would pay him an annual salary, provide him with benefits (health and life insurance), and allow him to participate in a 401(k) retirement program. This option would mean he would be working for the service all the time on various civil engineering projects. The position would require travel and living out of a suitcase. When one job ended, he would receive training to enhance his engineering skills. Martin opted for the staffing service position, because it would provide experience and training to keep him in demand.

Opportunities for the EngineeringTemp

MARTIN'S EXPERIENCE IS NOT UNIQUE, AS THE ENGINEERING PROFESsion makes ever-greater use of temporary staffing services to locate contract or temporary jobs and the expert personnel to perform those jobs. Due to unpredictable changes in the business cycle and the economy, more and more firms are using temporary engineering employees to meet their immediate short-term needs.

Another key factor in the increasing use of engineering temps is that engineering talent is also expensive talent. In today's environment, many firms are downsizing, "rightsizing," or reengineering to stay competitive. This means that they are aggressively looking for ways to cut costs and run lean. Because of the cyclic nature of most engineering projects, it becomes very expensive for firms to "warehouse" engineers between projects. It can be much more cost-effective to hire engineers for specific projects on a short-term basis. This is especially critical for small firms. Since the bulk of new job generation in the United States comes from small and growing companies, there is an enormous potential for temporary engineering services.

For these reasons, numerous staffing services now represent professional engineers, with Bernard Haldane Associates being one of the leaders with 71 offices nationwide. Other leading staffing services are SOS Technical Services and Science Temps, which has 20,000 engineers, scientists, and technicians listed with the service. The *National Business Employment Weekly* issue for June 22–28, 1997, featured "A Guide to Executive Temping," which included a directory of 100 agencies that place executive temps. Of the firms listed, the ones featuring engineers were: Career Marketing Associates Inc., CT Engineering Corporation, G/P Contract Staffing, International Staffing, Joulé Technical Staffing Inc., Sources Services Corporation, and The Whitaker Companies, Inc. For a more comprehensive listing, please refer to the Appendix of this book.

Engineering is a complex field encompassing the engineering disciplines historically taught in colleges and universities as well as the new types of engineering disciplines that teach people how to integrate their skills with those of people who work in information technology and with computers. The engineering disciplines typically—but not exclusively—include architectural, chemical, civil, electrical, industrial, and mechanical engineering. Each of these disciplines contains a subset of disciplines; for example, civil engineering can be further specialized into the areas of structural, environmental, geotechnical, sanitary, or transportation engineering. The broad category of electrical engineering also includes computer science with specialization in both hardware development and software. There are also technical skills that support the engineering disciplines—such as drafting or computer-aided design (CAD), surveying, and materials testing—that are represented by the firms placing engineers.

Industrial engineers work in quality control, design production systems, and study automation and operations. Materials engineers or metallurgical engineers work with plastics, metals, or artificial matter. One of the most popular fields is mechanical engineering, which involves working with machines. And, if you have drafting skills, many of the jobs you want are listed by those who place engineers. All of these skills in engineering can be applied to temporary professional technical jobs.

Types of Temporary Jobs Available

STAFFING SERVICE WEB SITES ON THE INTERNET SUGGEST A WIDE range of jobs available for engineers. Manpower Technical Services has an Engineering and Support category in its Technical Specialists area. Manpower's Web site (found at http://www.manpower.com) includes in the Engineering and Support category "Checkers, Design Engineers, Designers (CAD), Drafters (CAD), and Project Engineers."

The types of engineering positions that can be filled by the professional technical temp range from the technical (drafting or materials testing) to engineering management. Engineers can work independently on individual projects or as supervisors of projects and departments. Some staffing services work with one national client and send the professional technical engineer all over the country just to work for that client. Others recruit from a geographic region and cover a wide range of types of engineers. The demand for temporary engineering talent encompasses a wide range of disciplines and levels of experience.

A brief search of various Web sites on the Internet revealed the following types of jobs available for engineers: software/hardware engineers, Windows NT software engineers, UNIX software engineers, CAD designer, basic programmer, telecommunications, field application, mechanical, Oracle designer, software release, firmware, technical marketing, quality assurance, process, mechanical designer, manufacturing, principal, program management, and video software.

The pay for engineering services depends on supply and demand just as it does in other fields of business and professions. As a rule of thumb, the shorter the duration of the assignment or the higher the experience level, the higher the pay. It is also generally true that the more computer-literate you are and the wider the range of your experience, the more in demand you will be and the more pay you can command.

Computers

IF YOU CAN USE A COMPUTER, YOU WILL HAVE MORE OPPORTUNITIES to find the best-paying professional technical jobs, whether you want to be a full-time temporary or use temporary work to find a permanent job. Engineers now use computers to test how a system—a machine or a structure—will operate. Engineers also work with computerized drafters or those with CAD to forecast how designs will work. Working with computers is a trend in engineering that will continue to grow.

If you do not have computer skills, find a staffing service that will train you on the computer or take a computer class at a junior or community college or technical school so that you can earn more money. You will be competing with workers who have these computer skills and they will get the jobs you want unless you make the effort to acquire the skills. The various disciplines of engineering can be part of a team for project work, whether designing buildings or roads, and this project work is now integrated with computers. Engineering involves working with many changes in technology. Work with a staffing service that recognizes this. Some high-technology areas can become out-of-date or obsolete, or there may be an increase in the demand for very specialized skills. Like everything else, the engineering temp market is a matter of supply and demand.

Engineering Skills Used by Staffing Services

OTHER DISCIPLINES OF ENGINEERING COVERED BY THE STAFFING SERvices are ASIC (application-specific integrated circuits), CAD (computer-assisted drafting) specialists checkers, RF (radio frequency), digital/logic, test, verification, QA/QC (quality assurance/quality control), chemist/chemical, mask, math and modeling, aerospace designers, industrial, metallurgical, mining, nuclear, and petroleum.

Some of the types of engineering positions that can be filled by the professional/technical temp involve several different disciplines. Mechanical engineers can include engineering, design, and technicians. Electrical engineers include design and technicians. There are also chemical, design, industrial, quality, and process engineers.

Some of those skills recruited for electronic engineers are network application, network systems, and hardware. Chemical engineers recruited are those with management backgrounds, and with process design, process control, infrastructure process, and production and process skills.

A process engineer who wants to work as a technical professional temporary could be asked for chemical, process design, and process control systems experience. Someone who has infrastructure and production experience as well may be recruited all across the United States.

Mechanical engineers may need maintenance, infrastructure, and process experience as well as mechanical design experience.

+++

FIGURE 7.1 Bureau of Labor Statistics Salary Survey
for Engineers

Starting Salaries for Engineers with a Bachelor's Degree

Aerospace	$30,860
Chemical	39,204
Civil	29,809
Electrical	34,840
Industrial	33,267
Mechanical	35,051
Metallurgical	33,429
Mining	32,638
Nuclear	33,603
Petroleum	38,286

Median Annual Earnings for Various Levels of Engineers

Engineer I	$33,900
Engineer II	38,500
Engineer III	44,800
Engineer IV	54,400
Engineer V	65,400
Engineer VI	78,100
Engineer VII	90,000
Engineer VIII	105,700

Median Salaries for Some Engineering Specialties

Aerospace	$50,200
Chemical	53,100
Civil	44,700
Electrical	48,000
Industrial	40,900

Source: U.S. Department of Labor, Bureau of Labor Statistics. *Occupational Outlook Handbook, 1996–97 Edition.*

Drafters

AS MENTIONED EARLIER, DRAFTERS WORK ON MANY PROJECTS ON teams together with engineers as well as architects. Computer-aided drafting and design or CAD will continue to be a skill that is in demand more and more.

Many of the staffing services that recruit and place engineers and architects also place drafters on jobs. If you are a drafter looking for work as a temp or want to find full-time work as a temp-to-hire, search the Internet for Web sites of staffing services that place engineers.

The Bureau of Labor Statistics lists income for drafters who work year-round as averaging between $21,500 and $38,600, depending on experience, with the top 10% earning more than $50,200.

Bureau of Labor Statistics Salary Survey

THERE ARE MANY DISCIPLINES AND INDUSTRIES THAT SEARCH FOR engineers. Engineers can work at jobs from individual projects where they work independently up though being supervisors of departments and companies. Someone with engineering experience who does a search of Web sites on the Internet will find there are many opportunities to choose from in engineering. Figure 7.1 shows results of a Bureau of Labor Statistics survey of salaries for those in the engineering profession.

Again, refer to the formula for determining your pay as a temp as shown in Figure 3.1 on page 35.

CHAPTER EIGHT

Lawyers, Paralegals, and Legal Assistants

Why Law Firms and Legal Offices Need and Use Legal Temps

LAWYERS HOLD ABOUT 656,000 JOBS IN THE UNITED STATES. About three-fourths of the lawyers practice privately, either in law firms or in solo practices. Most of the remaining lawyers hold positions in government, the greatest number at the local level. Other lawyers are employed as house counsel by public utilities, banks, insurance companies, real estate agencies, manufacturing firms, welfare and religious organizations, and other business firms and nonprofit organizations. Some salaried lawyers also have part-time independent law practices; others work as lawyers part-time while working full-time in another occupation.

Law firms and legal organizations increasingly use both paralegals and attorneys as legal temps in many areas. For example, multidistrict litigation cases, class action lawsuits, major antitrust proceedings, wide-scale discrimination cases, some products liability cases, and major personal injury disaster cases (stemming from airplane crashes, explosions, mass food poisonings, rail derailments, ship or truck wrecks involving toxic chemicals, etc.) can occur in every state and impose extraordinary time and personnel demands on both plaintiff and defense law firms. Since by their very nature these litigation events are unpredictable, law firms cannot plan the deployment of their permanent full-time staff—thus necessitating the growing use of legal temps.

During pretrial discovery in such cases, tens of thousands and sometimes hundreds of thousands of computer files and paper files have to be examined by both plaintiff and defense law firms; thousands of witnesses have to be interviewed, and hundreds if not thousands of exhibits have to be prepared by each party's attorneys. This starts a chain reaction of time and energy requirements where, for example, the corporate law firm representing defendant corporations faces unexpected demands and needs additional staffing. Plaintiff's counsel often is a law firm or even a solo practitioner who is very proficient in the law but very limited in resources and staff.

In the Corrugated Box antitrust case tried in Houston in the late 1980s, every packaging container manufacturer and distributor in the United States was involved either as a party or as a potential witness in a case that lasted several years. In 1978, when a train carrying a boxcar of the toxic chemical Dioxin derailed near Centralia in Illinois, the resulting lawsuits numbered in the thousands and took seven years of actual court time to try. The IBM antitrust case in New York and the AT&T antitrust case in Washington, DC, took years to litigate and resolve. Currently, the dozens of class action lawsuits against the tobacco companies could be tried in court or could be settled at any time, as witness the settlement by Liggett Group Inc. in March 1997 and the summer 1997 settlement with nearly 40 state attorneys general.

When the plaintiffs' lawyers in class actions in Mississippi, Florida, and Louisiana (where the cigarette companies have been sued about the deleterious effects of tobacco) request hundreds of thousands of documents about cigarette research and marketing covering the years 1938 through 1994, defense counsel have no way to cope except through additional staff. In these kinds of cases, plaintiff's counsel and defense counsel have to expand their staff to handle these situations.

So both plaintiff's lawyers and defense lawyers need to employ additional legal staff such as attorneys and paralegals. Their choice is to retain them on a permanent basis or use temps. If the law firms hire a lot of legal full-time help, some of their worst nightmares could actually happen. What if the lawsuits are settled the week after they hire more full-time legal help? What if the discovery phase is suddenly limited by the judge and the court? What if a motion to dismiss the case is unexpectedly granted?

The law firms cannot retain permanent attorneys and paralegals for these purposes, since at the conclusion of the case—which can occur unexpectedly at any time (such as the recent tobacco settlements)—they would suddenly be overstaffed. Professional firms, such as lawyers, do not want to acquire a reputation for downsizing and professional layoffs, so they increasingly make use of legal temps.

Because of these problems and the concomitant explosion of litigation in the United States in the past 20 years, law firms face these staffing and hiring decisions every month.

Lawyers

MICHAEL Z. IS A 40-YEAR-OLD ATTORNEY WHO HAS BEEN PRACTICING law for 15 years in the Atlanta area. After he graduated from a prestigious law school he chose to join the corporate legal department of a major Atlanta bank. He moved up in the ranks of the legal department. The bank where he worked did very well and was acquired by an interstate bank holding company. But as a result of the acquisition, Michael Z. lost his job. The holding company that acquired his bank did not need two corporate legal departments, and Michael Z. was one of the lawyers who was downsized. He had been making approximately $60,000 in annual salary, about average for an in-house lawyer.

What did Michael Z. do next? While he enjoyed his severance package, he knew he did not have the luxury of taking early retirement. His family obligations required that he continue working and bringing an income to his family. The pressure was on. First, he arranged personal interviews with other banks in the area. While he did meet with them, there were no job offers. Then he tried interviewing with private law firms, only to learn that the law firms could hire recent law school graduates for half the salary he was asking.

Finally Michael Z. heard through a friend that one of the banks where he had applied for a job had been sued in a consumer credit class action and was going to hire additional legal help. He learned that instead of hiring full-time lawyers and paralegals for the lawsuit, the bank was going to hire through a legal staffing service.

The bank told Michael Z. they were using a nationally based legal staffing service, so he made an appointment with the service. He submitted his resume, filled out an application, and requested legal work at the bank. After checking his references and verifying he was licensed to practice law, the staffing service ran a background check on him. Michael Z. was hired by the legal staffing service and sent to work at the bank a week later, as soon as it was determined there were no ethical conflicts of interest. He made $33 an hour and worked for the staffing service for almost a year while he continued to interview for other permanent employment.

In addition to the unpredictability of staffing needs, law firms are trying to maximize their profit margins at a time when clients, especially large corporate clients, are resisting any increase in hourly billing rates. The alternative then is for the law firms to reduce their costs, and one solution is the expanded use of legal temps who will never make partner and who don't expect to be paid at partner rates. As the *Tampa Tribune* reported on July 14, 1996, in a story about professional temping jobs, "Even law firms, operating in the stuffiest and most tradition-bound of businesses, have explored temporary staffing. Strapped by stalling billing hours, the firms resist hiring attorneys except when they need to." The easy solution in the past 20 years has been to expand the development of legal temps and legal staffing services. Companies such as Amicus Legal Staffing, Inc., with offices in 8 states and plans for expansion to 16 more states in the near future, provide both lawyers and paralegals who assist in these situations on a temporary basis.

Lawyers who work as temporary lawyers through staffing services should expect to be paid about $25 to $30 per hour on the average if they have relatively little experience. Experienced lawyers who work as temporaries could expect to make $20 to $45 per hour more. Factors affecting the rate of pay include: experience, academic record, type of practice, size of employer, location of employer, and the specialized legal knowledge desired. The field of law makes a difference, too.

Thus, depending on the region of the country and the experience of the legal temp, an attorney seeking temp work could expect to be paid in the range of $25 per hour to $75 per hour, meaning that the professional staffing service will charge its customer $35 to $100 per hour. A paralegal temp can expect to earn about $15 to $20 per hour.

Various staffing services, such as Amicus Legal Staffing, LAW/ Temps, The Wallace Law Registry, and Lawyers Lawyer, have greatly increased the marketing for corporate legal departments and law firms that desire to employ attorneys on a temporary basis. Many of these temporary attorneys are persons who have not yet taken or passed the bar examination but are still qualified to carry out significant legal responsibilities. Many have young children and need flexibility with their home life, or have moved to a new area to accommodate their spouse's career. Others have retired from full-time positions and are simply slowing down their professional life.

Paralegal and Legal Assistant Temps

MANY PERSONS COULD QUALIFY FOR PARALEGAL AND LEGAL ASSISTANT staffing jobs. One of the fastest-growing areas of professional temporary employment is that of paralegals and assistants working for law firms, corporate legal departments, and the government.

According to the Bureau of Labor Statistics, the use of paralegals and legal assistants has expanded over 100% in the past decade and now exceeds 100,000 jobs. While some states are now considering licensing requirements for paralegals, paralegals and legal assistants are usually nonlicensed personnel who perform routine tasks for lawyers. For example, paralegals interview witnesses; prepare documents such as real estate closing statements, Uniform Commercial Code filings, litigation checklists, and trial exhibits; prepare bankruptcy schedules; and perform other work that allows the attorney to devote her or his time to more complex functions. Many paralegals graduate from a paralegal school. Usually no college degree is required, although it may be helpful. If you choose to attend a paralegal school, make sure it is certified by the American Bar Association or the American Association of Law Schools, as that may help your job placement opportunities.

Lawyers, assisted by paralegals and legal assistants, act as both advocates and advisers in our society. As advocates, they represent one of the opposing parties in criminal and civil trials by presenting evidence that supports their client in court. As advisers, lawyers counsel their clients as to their legal rights and obligations, and suggest particular courses of action in business and personal matters. Whether acting as advocates or advisers, all attorneys interpret the law and apply it to specific situations. This requires excellent research and communication skills, and frequently the research and initial preparation will be assigned to a paralegal.

In-depth research is performed into the purposes behind the applicable laws and into judicial decisions that have been applied to those laws under circumstances similar to those currently faced by the client. While all lawyers and paralegals continue to make use of law libraries to prepare cases, many supplement their search of the conventional printed sources with computer software packages. Software can be used to automatically search legal literature and identify legal texts relevant to a specific case or problem. In litigation involving many supporting documents, paralegals will use computers to organize and index the material. Law firms specializing in tax law are increasingly using computers for making tax computations and exploring alternative tax strategies for clients.

Paralegal temps report to the lawyers about their research and the lawyers then communicate to others the information obtained by research. They advise what actions clients may take and draw up legal documents, such as wills and contracts, for clients.

The majority of paralegal temps are in private practice where they may assist lawyers on criminal or civil law. In criminal law, lawyers represent individuals who have been charged with crimes and argue their cases. In civil law, they assist clients with litigation, wills, trusts, contracts, mortgages, titles, and leases.

Paralegal temps are often used by lawyers who are employed full-time by a single client. If the client is a corporation, the lawyer is known as house counsel and usually advises the company about legal issues related to its business activities. These issues might involve patents, government regulations, contracts with other companies, property interests, or collective bargaining agreements with unions.

Paralegal temps also work for government legal staffs, and attorneys employed at the various levels of government make up still another category. Lawyers who work for state attorneys general, prosecutors, public defenders, and courts play a key role in the criminal justice system. At the federal level, attorneys investigate cases for the Department of Justice, Department of the Treasury, or other agencies. Also, paralegals assist lawyers at every government level to help develop programs, draft laws, interpret legislation, and establish enforcement procedures on behalf of the government.

Other lawyers work for legal aid societies—private nonprofit organizations established to serve disadvantaged people. These lawyers generally handle civil rather than criminal cases. Government funding for legal aid organizations has been slashed in recent years, so, like private law firms, they are trying to curtail their costs by making more use of staffing services.

Temp Employment

THERE SHOULD BE STEADY GROWTH IN THE FUTURE FOR TEMPORARY legal jobs. The Bureau of Labor Statistics calculates that there will be faster-than-average growth in the legal market. Traditionally, the demand for legal temps is constant or expanding, since when the national economy is growing there will be a need for legal services to help businesses grow and when the national economy is stagnant there is an increased need for bankruptcy and debtor-creditor legal work.

Earnings

SPECIAL COUNSEL IS ONE OF THE NATION'S LARGEST STAFFING SERVICES specializing in the placement of lawyers and paralegals. Joe D. Freedman, president and CEO of Amicus Legal Staffing, now a part of Special Counsel, a division of Accustaff Staffing Services, offers the following observation: More and more members of the legal profession, including attorneys and paralegals, are choosing to work for staffing firms like Special Counsel because of the quality of life that being a temp, legal contractor worker, or consultant can offer.

There are two types of people who come into a legal staffing service like Amicus: those with three to five years of legal experience, and recent law school graduates. Experienced people are used to working 60- to 70-hour weeks and producing a lot of billable hours for a law firm. They may have made partner or not made partner. They are tired of the rat race of the typical law firm and are looking for a different lifestyle. The lifestyle they want may be a full-time job in another law firm where they can work 40 hours and make a good salary. The other option may be to work on various projects as a legal temp or contractor for a staffing service.

Therefore, according to Freedman, the typical experienced legal temp is either looking for a temp-to-hire type of situation through Special Counsel or wants to be kept busy working for a variety of clients where the temp is placed by Special Counsel.

Over 80% of the legal temps who come to Special Counsel are looking for a permanent job. A tryout program where Special Counsel sends the lawyer or paralegal to a firm for a probation period of several weeks or months is especially popular with the legal temp because it not only allows the business where the temp is working to try out the temp for a period of time, but, more importantly, it allows the temp to see if this is where he or she wants to spend the next several years being a lawyer or a paralegal. Remember, everyone can be on one's best behavior for a couple of weeks, but it takes a full-moon cycle to show someone's true colors; that goes not only for the temp but, more importantly, for the business where the temp is working.

A lawyer who has been unhappy with a big corporate firm and is placed at another large firm as a temp can decide whether that is really where he or she wants to work next. Or will the lawyer be getting into the same type of atmosphere that he or she is trying to get away from?

The other type of candidate who comes to a company like Special Counsel is the recent law school graduate. Freedman says staffing services will look at where the graduate placed in the class. Candidates who are in the upper half of the graduating class have a greater chance of being placed. But if you were not in the upper half, do not be discouraged! Freedman said staffing services also look at work experience. For example, if you worked in a bank before or during law school, a staffing service may be able to place you on an assignment that would utilize not only your banking skills but also your legal education.

The trend in legal staffing, according to Freedman, is to provide two types of services. The first is traditional temping or placement. That means someone calls a service like Special Counsel and needs a lawyer or a paralegal for a specific amount of time strictly as a temporary employee. The other type of service, traditional staffing, is when a company calls Special Counsel and needs someone who will be a full-time employee. The company will either pay a fee up front to Special Counsel, which is called a direct placement, or will try someone out for a period of time while paying Special Counsel by the hour for this person's skills.

Outsourcing is an area of legal staffing that is really growing, according to Freedman. Many law firms now call a staffing service when they have a big project to handle, whether they need research done or they need preparation completed for litigation. Rather than add to their head count, they call a staffing service and tell the staffing service to handle the project. The project could last for a month to several years. The staffing service must then recruit and manage the legal work done for this special project. Handing out these projects to an outsider is called outsourcing. The legal staff for these projects work as a part of a law firm but are employees of the staffing service.

When asked what characteristics qualify someone to be a successful legal temp, Freedman said those who have practiced law for five years and were graduated from an American Bar Association–accredited law school are qualified. The candidate will need to work in urban areas as opposed to small towns. These people also need to be Internet-savvy. Over 85% of the resumes come to Freedman via e-mail.

Computer skills are important to the legal temp. Persons who have Windows experience and can type their own letters and memos are more placeable. Many legal temps are also using laptops. The legal temp should also be proficient in using the computer for legal research. Recent law school graduates will know how to use the computer. If you are not computer-literate and fairly skilled in the use of computers, all research indicates you should take the time to learn.

The immediate growth trends in legal staffing, according to Freedman, are in intellectual property work, litigation, and corporate work.

Staffing services that hire members of the legal profession are like other staffing services that recruit the professional technical temp. These white-collar staffing services are offering benefits for temps that are very competitive. Items such as health insurance, 401(k), credit unions, and referral bonuses are offered to those who are working temp while looking for full-time work as well as those who are looking to become a permanent temp or full-time employee of the staffing service.

Shelley Wallace, president of The Wallace Law Registry, the nation's largest legal placement firm and a subsidiary of Kelly Services, Inc., offers this suggestion to lawyers or paralegal professionals interested in temporary employment: only register with a reputable agency, an agency managed by attorneys—one that is local, has been around for awhile, and knows the marketplace. She also says that even if you are really looking for a permanent position, a temp job might be an ideal way for a prospective employer to evaluate your performance before making a long-term commitment.

CHAPTER NINE

Choosing the Right Staffing Service

NOW THAT YOU HAVE DECIDED TO TAKE ADVANTAGE OF THE OP-portunities available to a temporary professional, executive, or technical employee, how do you go about choosing which staffing service or services you will work for? (You can work with several at the same time.)

Several things can guide your selection process, including Internet information, referrals from people you know who are temping or have worked with a staffing services in the past, the reputation of the staffing service, friendliness of the staff, convenience, pay, flexibility, benefits, location, the type of job you are looking for, and whether the staffing service is employer- or employee-paid. Your career goals and where you want to work are also important.

The Internet

PERHAPS NO OTHER WAY OF JOB SEARCHING FOR BOTH TEMPORARY and permanent professional technical jobs is growing as fast as the Internet. Many people are surfing the Net as a way to discover what is out there in terms of jobs and opportunities. Staffing services that place people in both permanent and temporary technical professional jobs have Web sites on the Internet. Many of the staffing services in the Appendix have Web sites, and those that do not may be in the process of developing sites.

The Internet is changing the way employers and prospective employees (in this case, professional technical temps) interact or communicate with each other. The Web sites of some staffing services will have a series of options that are user-friendly to guide you to the location of the office nearest you. Other Web sites will give you an option of communicating directly with the service through e-mail. You can even complete a resume that is keyword-driven and send it to a staffing service through the Internet. The service can also correspond with you by e-mail should you decide to give a staffing service your e-mail address.

Using a Web site can save you, the professional technical temp, a lot of time. You do not have to stay on hold while a receptionist is trying to find someone to talk to you. You can narrow your search of staffing services by deciding which ones have the technical savvy to operate via the Internet. You can also make your job search as a prospective temporary or full-time employee as narrow or as wide as you want to by listing preferences as to where you want to work. Many staffing services that list temporary part-time and full-time jobs on the Internet indicate where the jobs are. That way, the staffing service hopes to recruit temps who want to work in those areas. Why respond to a job in Alaska when you only want to work in Hawaii?

International and National Staffing Services

HOW ARE THE BIG NATIONAL AND INTERNATIONAL STAFFING FIRMS recruiting and placing professional technical temporaries? In interviews with Kelly Services, Manpower, and Robert Half Accountemps, here is what their spokespersons said:

Carl Camden, Executive Vice President of Kelly Services in charge of Sales and Marketing, said Kelly Services uses the Internet widely. Camden thinks over 70% of Kelly Services' recruits are a result of the Internet. The Web site (address: http://www.kellyservices.com) lists the types of jobs available and the skills needed.

Kelly Services also has a site that will build a resume for the professional technical person. This will help the candidate make sure the resume is formatted so that the correct key words will be included.

As mentioned in Chapter 4, this is important because many services use scanners that are programmed to select candidates based on how the scanner is coded. Therefore, it is important that you make sure your skills are listed correctly on your resume according to the temp part-time or full-time job you are applying for. Your resume then has a greater chance of being selected by a programmed scanner.

If you have any questions about why your resume was not selected, call the staffing service you submitted it to and ask to talk to a real, live person who can give you an explanation. Computers are only as good as the commands given them. You may be qualified for a job that a person from a staffing service can select you for even though your resume may not have been selected by a computer. It never hurts to be persistent and to follow up on each and every listed job for which you may be qualified.

In an interview, Gretchen Kreske, manager of strategic information for Manpower, said Manpower has been placing people in professional technical jobs for over 25 years. Manpower recruits extensively from its Internet site at http://www.manpower.com, and one of the programs offered by Manpower, according to Kreske, is TechTrack. TechTrack is Manpower's CD-based technical training for information technology professionals.

One way to use the Internet is to enter the type of job you are looking for and review the Web sites that match your skills. Or, you can type in the name of a staffing service and review what the Web site lists. For example, if you type in the Robert Half Accountemps Web site at http://www.accountemps.com, you will be offered a variety of options. The options include locations of the Robert Half Accountemps office closest to you, the types of skills Accountemps is recruiting for, jobs available with salaries, and where the jobs are located.

Mark Nightingale, with Robert Half Accountemps, said many applicants come from referrals: "Good people know good people." Many people with professional technical skills come to Accountemps via the Internet, and some come because of the special kinds of financial jobs where Robert Half Accountemps has a reputation for placing the professional technical temporary.

Many Web sites will also allow you to send the initial information to the staffing service through the Internet. That means you can complete an application and fax your resume to the number listed on the site. You may be asked questions by e-mail or by a phone call if you give your name and number.

Joanie was an information technology specialist who found herself looking for work because the company she worked for had been sold and the national company that had acquired her company had foolishly done away with the information technology division. (This company obviously had no vision since they abolished the information technology division, and Joanie was better off not working for them.) While Joanie was living off her severance pay, she starting surfing the Net to see what else was out there as far as jobs went.

Joanie found many staffing services listed on the Web. She had to determine which staffing services recruited candidates like her who had technical skills. After narrowing her search down to 12 services, she carefully read the job openings listed on their Web sites. Some of the services had functions that allowed her to fill in a resume format and actually send the resume through the Internet to the service. She tried three of these services and, following their instructions, entered her job skills according to their format.

She listed an e-mail address as well as a phone number where she could be reached. Rather than give out her home phone number, Joanie listed the number of an outplacement service that her previous company had contracted to provide office support for the people who were downsized, fired, or simply laid off.

Joanie received responses from two of the staffing services that she sent resumes to through the Internet. One response was by e-mail and one was by phone. The e-mail response asked specific questions about the different programming languages with which she was familiar and her willingness to relocate and travel. The phone call was to ask more specific questions about her skill development.

The person who contacted her by phone was very abrasive and abrupt. Since Joanie was at a rather vulnerable time in her life, this did not sit well with her. The e-mail contact was direct but also left the door open for Joanie to respond and ask more questions. The information shared in e-mail covered aspects of what Joanie was looking for in a job, whether she was interested in long-term temping, what types of benefits she wanted, and whether she wanted a temp-to-hire job. Joanie was not sure what she wanted at this point, although she basically wanted to avoid the type of position she had just left. She did not want to be a part of shortsighted company, so she responded that she wanted to be flexible and not lock herself into anything that was long-term, meaning longer than three to six months for her. (In the world of temp, long-term can mean years to never-ending.)

The staffing service person Joanie had been conversing with by e-mail set up a phone interview with her and explained the type of position the staffing service was trying to fill.

One job was an information technology position lasting approximately six months, and the pay was what Joanie was asking for. The contact from the staffing service went on to say she would need to have a background check run on her for the job and pass a series of tests. The job assignment turned out to be a win-win for Joanie.

She took her first job as a professional temp with this service as a result of finding it on the Internet. She went on to work other jobs through two other staffing services she had found on the Internet and eventually tried out a temp-to-hire job. At present, Joanie is still uneasy about committing herself to one company due to her past experience, but now she knows if the job does not work out she can go back to professional temping.

In her spare time, Joanie continues to surf the Net to stay informed about jobs available for someone with her skills. She is considering picking up some weekend temp work to sharpen her information technology skills and to earn extra income.

Referrals—Ask Your Friends Who Temp

ASK A LOT OF QUESTIONS WHEN CHOOSING A SERVICE. IF YOU HAVE friends who have worked temp, ask them what staffing service they work for and how they have been treated by the staffing service. How you are treated should be a leading factor when choosing a staffing service. Many services that work with professional technical temps recruit a majority of their employees by referrals. They may even offer a cash bonus to temps who refer other professional temps to them.

In addition to recruits who have used the Internet, Kelly Services' staffing service also finds candidates through two other ways. Referrals from other candidates are the second biggest source, after the Internet. Someone who is working for Kelly Services who has a good experience will send, or refer, someone else to Kelly Services. It is similar to going out on a blind date—you are more receptive to going out with someone a friend has set you up with or referred you to because you value and trust that friend's judgment. The same thing applies working for a staffing service—you feel better about signing up with a service a friend has had a good experience with rather than trying to find a service on your own.

The third way Kelly Services finds professional technical temps is through advertising. Kelly Services places ads for jobs to be filled in newspapers and in professional journals. If you read Kelly Services' ads you will see they are recruiting for lawyers (the company is one of the largest employers of temporary lawyers in the world), engineers, accountants, information technology professionals, and, as mentioned earlier, scientists.

When asked why so many professional technical people are working through Kelly Services rather than finding a traditional full-time job, Carl Camden, Executive Vice President in charge of Sales and Marketing, said that more people prefer the Kelly Services style of working. That means, according to Camden, more professionals would rather have the flexibility of interim work. When surveyed, over 40% of Kelly Services' professional technical temps said they would not take a permanent job if offered one.

Camden said another reason the professional technical industry has grown so much is because companies turn to Kelly Services to complete project work. For example, a company needs a project requiring a specific information technology skill. If the company trains one of its permanent people to do the job, that requires time and capital. If it recruits someone on its own with the skill, that again requires the time and cost to recruit the person (place the ad, screen the resume, test the person, etc.) or have the in-house human resource department find the person.

Camden says if the company calls Kelly Services, then Kelly Services can find the appropriate professional to do the work. After the Kelly Services person finishes the job at the company, then Kelly Services will place that same information technology person somewhere else. If the company did not use a service like Kelly Services to source this skill, at the end of the project the company would have to fire or keep the information technology person on the permanent staff. So, this saves money for the company, because the company does not have the information technology person on its payroll after the job is over. The company does not have to train the information technology person for the job, because Kelly Services sends someone in who knows the job and can start doing the job right away without extensive training. The project people provided by Kelly Services go away from the companies where they have done the work and on to other Kelly Services jobs at other companies.

The fringe benefits that Kelly Services offers its temps are like those of many other big staffing services. There is a wide variety or menu of benefits available. For more information, contact the nearest Kelly Services staffing service or review the Web site at http://www.kellyservices.com.

Reputation—Who Pays the Fee?

REMEMBER, A TEMPORARY EMPLOYEE IS JUST AS VALUABLE TO THE staffing service as the business where the staffing service places the temp on the job. A staffing service must have both temporary employees and clients to send them to on jobs in order to be successful. If a staffing service cannot bring the temps and clients together, it cannot accomplish its goal. If a staffing service does not value you as a temporary employee, stop working with it and switch to a staffing service that does value its temps.

For example, Banking Staffing Service may have a great working relationship with the bank that hires the staffing service to fill temp orders for the bank. But, if Banking Staffing Service does not have the same excellent working relationship with its temps, it cannot be successful, because it will not have a product (temps) to sell the bank. Banking Staffing Service must be friendly and cooperative with the temporary employees in order to find people to send to the bank. Make sure you select a staffing service that values and treats temps with respect.

What kind of reputation does the staffing service have? Do you have any friends who have temped? If so, what staffing services did they like to work for? Many staffing services give a referral bonus to temps for recruiting other temps. Find out what staffing services your friends like to temp for and why.

Choose only a staffing service that is employer-paid. You never want to work for a staffing service where it will cost you money to find a job. There are too many staffing services that will not charge you looking for temps for you to need to work with the others.

Convenience

HOW IMPORTANT IS CONVENIENCE TO YOU? DOES THE STAFFING SERVICE need to be close to you geographically or just on-line? Are their help desks actually helpful? In other words, if you need help away about a job you are on or a problem you are having, is there someone readily available to help or give you an answer? Can you easily reach someone on the phone? Does the service make you feel like you are the most important customer they have? Or, does it take forever to get an answer? The good services will go out of their way to make you feel important. They should be smart enough to know if they do not help you, you will go work for another service and therefore make another staffing service money.

Will you work with several people from one staffing service at the same time, or will you be assigned one person who is responsible for keeping you busy? Do you like working with more than one person at a service, or do you prefer a service where you will be given a lot of individual attention? In other words, do you prefer impersonal, infrequent attention, or does your personality style enjoy a lot of attention?

What geographic area do you want to work in? Are you limited as to where you can work, or can you go anywhere? If you are limited, make sure you find a staffing service that places temps in the area where you must work.

Working with Several Staffing Services at the Same Time

YOU MAY WANT TO CHOOSE SEVERAL SERVICES TO WORK WITH AT THE same time. The advantages are that you may work more frequently, be paid more, and have more variety in your temp assignments.

The disadvantages are that you may not be able to accrue benefits with a staffing service unless you work at least one thousand hours a year. Many staffing services offer vacation benefits to temps who work that many hours a year.

Working with Only One Staffing Service

IF YOU WORK WITH ONE STAFFING SERVICE, YOU MAY BUILD A CLOSE relationship with the service staff and as a result you may be sent on the better jobs. By working with one staffing service, you will be letting the service get to know your likes and dislikes and where you work best. The staffing service should then only send you on the premium jobs.

There are advantages and disadvantages in temping through one or multiple staffing services. In summary, the advantages to working with one staffing service are that the staffing service will get to know your preferences, you will be more than just a number, you can accrue benefits, and your loyalty should be rewarded by your being sent on the very best jobs. The disadvantage is you will be limited to working only in the businesses that use that particular staffing service. You will miss out working at companies that use other staffing services.

If you want to work temp for long periods of time or you want to earn your income as a temp and not as a permanent employee, consider the advantages of working with one service. You can get benefits and have access to many insurance plans.

If you have a special skill like accounting or legal expertise, you will want to work with services that specialize in placing accountants or lawyers. That way you will be sent on jobs that match your specific skills. You will also probably earn more money working through a staffing service that recruits and places only in information technology, accounting and finance, healthcare, scientific, engineering, or legal fields.

Professional Technical Staffing Services versus General Staffing Services

SOME STAFFING SERVICES ARE FORMED TO STAFF ONLY PROFESSIONAL and technical temps. They have come about as a result of the need for people with specific skills. Examples are Accountemps for accounting, Amicus for legal, and Maxwell Medical for medical skills. Other general staffing services started several years ago to create professional technical divisions within their companies as a result of the phenomenal growth in the professional technical sector of the staffing industry. Examples of these are Manpower, which created Manpower Technical; Kelly Services, which created Kelly Services Technical; Olsten, which now has Olsten Accounting, Legal, and Healthcare; and Accustaff, which has Special Counsel.

There is no easy way to select a staffing service. Remember, the staffing service business is the second-fastest-growing industry worldwide, second only to the computer industry. Professional technical placement is the fastest-growing part of the staffing business. As a result, more and more staffing services are specializing in specific placement of temps or consultants who have the professional technical skills that are in demand. There are services that place only those with computer skills; there are services for engi-

110

neers, for nurses, for hospital technicians, for accounting and finance. And, more staffing services are now being developed to address the demand for these technical and professional skills on a temporary basis or on a temp-to-hire basis. The good staffing services will stay in business. The bad ones that do not know what they are doing or who are unethical will hopefully be put out of business, because no one wants to temp for them or hire skills through them.

The procedure for finding a staffing service is going to be different for every person. It is going to require effort, work, and patience on your part as you test each service.

The smart staffing services know that they have to have a product to make money. The product is you, the professional temp. The smart staffing service will try to be as user-friendly as possible. That is why you will see a lot of options in the Internet that make signing up with services as fast and as easy as possible.

You may try to sign up with some staffing services that are geared toward very specific skills like engineering, accounting, legal, information technology, healthcare, and science. You would also be smart to sign up with some of the big general staffing firms like Manpower, Kelly Services, StaffMark, Robert Half, Accustaff, Adecco, and Olsten and work through their specific technical divisions such as information technology, accounting, and medical.

Staffing services tell you in their advertising what skills they are looking for. These skills may be made known in printed advertising, on the Internet, or through the referrals of the people they are currently working. Remember, if someone you know has skills similar to yours and seems happy working for a staffing service, ask for the name of the service. Your friend may be paid a referral fee for sending you to the service. You may also pull up the Web sites on the Internet for various services. Most staffing services' sites have a space for you to enter the skill you want to use. For example, when you type in the skill "legal research," the site will list what offices are staffing paralegals and list the job openings that match your skills, or it may tell you, "Sorry, no matches."

Remember, if you have a very specific technical skill, take the time to do some investigative work and find out which staffing services place people with your skills and where you can maximize your abilities or earn the most money.

Investigate

THE WAY TO DO INVESTIGATIVE WORK IS TO USE SEVERAL RESOURCES. Surf the Internet. Call your local chamber of commerce and get a listing of all the services. Check the yellow pages or phone book. Check professional organizations. Don't forget about asking the personnel offices of the companies you have an interest in working for. Read the classified section of your local newspapers (many staffing services recruit only in the Sunday or weekend edition of the local paper).

Check other periodicals in your community and always check out the library. Read the ads in the papers or directories and see what types of advertising different services do.

What types of positions are staffing services recruiting for? Look in the newspaper and see which services are hiring for what kinds of jobs. Many times, services list the pay for these jobs in their ads.

The yellow pages often have big display ads for staffing services. In these display ads there will be a lot of information about the staffing service, including where the service is located, what types of jobs they hire temps for, and sometimes the area of town they service.

Another point of reference is industry publications. If you are an accountant, engineer, computer operator, or in the healthcare or legal profession, check your publications and see what services advertise in them.

Many technical schools and colleges have worked with services in placing their students. Ask the placement counselors at those institutions what services are good to work with.

Recruiting personnel in the military also refer to staffing services candidates who are waiting to be inducted. This way the military can keep their candidates working and productive after they have enlisted and are waiting to report for duty. Ask military recruiters what services are good to work with.

Call staffing services on the phone and talk to them. First of all, how prepared are the services on the phone? If they are not professional on the phone, do not waste your time temping for them. Chances are, they will not be professional to work with, either.

You may not know it is a common practice for staffing services to "shop" each other. That means services send in staff members to see how professional competitors are and what types of services they offer their temps. Do the same thing. Shop the staffing services for yourself. Make sure you are being treated as a valued customer. You do it all the time when you are shopping for a tailor, hairdresser, clothing store, dry cleaner—and some even do it when looking for a place of worship! Why shouldn't you shop around when you are selecting a staffing service that could land you your next job?

In order to be placed on a temp job as a computer specialist, you need to find a service that recruits and places temps with those skills. Some services list their pay rates for temps in their ads or will tell you on the phone what they are. Other services will ask you to come in and be evaluated before they tell you what they can pay you.

If there is a business where you want to work that does not have any current openings but does use an employment service for staffing needs, ask the business what service is used. Then sign up with that service and ask to be placed on any temporary jobs that service may have available at that particular business.

There are countless success stories where someone has gotten a start at a company as a temporary employee. Dan was placed in the mailroom at a music recording company on a temporary assignment. He worked very hard, showed a lot of initiative and commitment, and was hired full-time by the company. Dan eventually was named as the human resources person at that recording company. That meant Dan was the person who was given the authority to call staffing services when the music company needed temporary part-time and full-time employee assistance. Dan's story was a win-win for Dan, the music company, and the staffing service. It was smart on the part of the staffing service to make Dan feel important and valued, because Dan turned out to be the decision maker for the music company as to which staffing service was going to receive the recording company's annual staffing business of approximately $250,000.

If the staffing service had not treated Dan well, he could have chosen to give the music company's business to another staffing service. People who are temps today often turn into the order placers of tomorrow in the world of professional technical staffing. That is another reason it is important for you to choose a service where you feel valued and are treated fairly. You may be given the authority to choose a service in the future, and you will want to work with a service where you have had a good experience. If Dan had not been treated well by the staffing service who placed him at the music company, he would have gone out of his way to make sure he never had to work with that service again.

Independent versus National and International Staffing Services

EVERY PERSON IS DIFFERENT. YOU NEED TO SELECT A STAFFING SERVICE or several services that work well for you. You may rarely talk to your service or you may have contact with them every week. A staffing service that meets your needs now may not be in the position to meet your needs next year. This means a service may pay you well, offer you great benefits today, and keep you challenged with great jobs. But next year that staffing service may lose some major contracts with clients they service and may then not have as many jobs to offer you.

Services can be either locally owned or part of a national or international chain. Examples of international services are Manpower and Adecco (formerly Adia), operating both in the United States and overseas. The big staffing services may have contracted with international corporations because big companies with offices in many cities often choose a vendor, in this case a staffing service, that has lots of locations in multiple cities. Examples of these services are Kelly Services, Manpower, and Olsten. All of the major staffing services are listed in the Appendix to this book.

Large staffing services offer advantages to temps who need to move. You can fill out an application with a national staffing service and it can transfer your temp records by computer from city to city. Your records will include your area of expertise, the type of jobs you like, and what you need to be paid.

Some big companies may have contracts with national staffing services. This means these companies have an agreement to use the same national service in all their offices throughout the country. Even though a corporation has an agreement with a national service, it does not mean the corporation will use the same service from city to city. In other words, there are exceptions to every rule. Many corporations will allow a local office to use a staffing service other than the service the corporation has a contract with.

Services that are locally owned are independent and not part of a chain. The temporary industry has grown so fast that many people have started small temp services to meet the growing need for temps. As a result, there are many cities that have excellent locally owned temporary services. Both large and small technical staffing services offer Internet services that will allow you to sign up on-line or submit your resume by e-mail.

If a locally owned service has the best reputation in your community, that is the service you should pick. You may get more individualized attention by working with a locally owned service.

Many large international companies may choose a few small technical staffing services to find technical and professional temps or consultants to work on projects at these large companies. This means some small information technology staffing firms, engineering services, or accounting specialists may spend all their time recruiting temps for a few major clients. A large company may find it receives better service from a small technical staffing service as opposed to locking in to a national staffing service.

For example, International Q Company selected Small Staffing

Specialists to fill its information technology temp and full-time jobs because Small Staffing is located in the Silicon Valley area of California and has access to many people who stay up-to-date on the latest information technology. If Small Staffing cannot fill the jobs, it sources another staffing service to be a backup. When the other staffing service finds a qualified person, it works through Small Staffing, which "tiers" or handles all of the staffing needs for International Q Company. Any service that sends people who are information technology temps to International Q sends them through Small Staffing, which in turn keeps all of the paperwork and controls the invoices for the information technology temps working at International Q. International Q likes this arrangement because the tier staffing cuts down on its paperwork, and Small Staffing likes it because the service can control the work of the information technology temps even if Small Staffing does not find and recruit all of the information technology temps who work at International Q.

You can expect to see more of this working together or tier arrangement by several staffing services to take care of a big client. This is because there are some skills that are in great demand and often just one staffing service cannot find enough people who have these skills. Therefore, several services will work together to find the skilled workers. This should be a win-win for the professional technical temp who has the skills that are in demand.

How flexible are you regarding travel and relocation? Do you want to stay in your community and commute for the day and come home at night? If so, some of the staffing services located in your hometown may offer jobs that fit this lifestyle. Do not overlook both the independent or locally owned and the big international staffing services where you live. There is no consistency from city to city about what staffing service fills what orders. Just because a staffing service fills a job for a company in Milwaukee does not mean the same staffing service fills the same kind of jobs for the same company in San Diego.

Do your investigative work when choosing a staffing service. Again, check reputation and make sure the service always pays its temps on time.

What Happens If You Pick the Wrong Staffing Service?

BETH HAD A VERY BAD EXPERIENCE WITH BRAND Z SERVICE. SHE went to work for that staffing service and was punctual in reporting for work. She also turned in her hours when she was supposed to. But, when Beth went to pick up her paycheck, it was not there.

What Beth did not know was that Brand Z Service had a terrible reputation for dealing with its temporary employees. Brand Z would be very nice to the businesses it sent temps to but treated the temps like they were just a number, not a valuable part of the business. Beth did not receive a paycheck because Brand Z did not take the time to write her a check, nor did the company care that she had financial obligations to meet. When Brand Z finally did give Beth her paycheck, it bounced! Brand Z was having financial problems and had a notorious reputation in the community for financial instability.

What Happens When You Investigate and Select the Right Staffing Service?

BE LIKE TOM INSTEAD. WHEN TOM DECIDED TO BECOME A TEMP, HE called his local chamber of commerce and got a list of staffing services from them. He then reviewed the Internet, the yellow pages, and the newspapers for advertising. He saw a few ads that attracted his interest in the jobs they were recruiting for.

He then called three staffing services and asked questions about their ads. Two services even said they could pay him what he was asking for if he tested to meet their qualifications.

Tom is now temping through two services. One keeps him busy most of the time and the other still calls him to offer him jobs. He has no problem getting paid on time and has been placed at reputable companies. One of the services is a locally owned independent service and the other is a national service.

The locally owned service works Tom the most as a customer service representative at banks from 8:00 A.M. to 5:00 P.M. Monday through Friday. The national service keeps Tom busy when he wants to work evenings and weekends supervising the market polling that the national service has a contract for.

How to Find the Right Staffing Service— The Professional Technical Temp's Expectations

IN TODAY'S STRESSFUL AND COMPLEX WORK ENVIRONMENT, MANY professional workers suffer burnout—that is, dissatisfaction with their high-stress jobs, lack of fulfillment in their professional lives, and increasingly a sense of restlessness and regret as to the professional careers they have chosen.

Marketing studies and polls consistently show that these professionals, especially many attorneys and healthcare workers, desire less stress in their work and would change careers if they could. The same problems afflict recent graduates. Among law school graduates in 1996, 10% did not pursue jobs in the legal profession, according to the National Association for Law Placement; and the trend is pronouncedly upwards, as less than 5% of law school graduates eight years earlier in 1988 did not seek legal careers. Approximately one-fourth of law school graduates now work in employment positions where a law degree is not required.

One result of these frustrations centered around stress, boredom, and burnout is that an ever-growing number of professional and technical employees are entering the temporary employment market as an alternative. Combined with the professional and technical employees who are involuntarily downsized and outplaced, these highly trained professional and technical employees are the future of the staffing services business. Many of them can be placed by staffing services in their field of expertise where they continue to practice law, medicine, accounting, or architecture. At the same time many other professionals can and will be placed in executive positions such as human resources management, administration, or planning so as to utilize their talent and experience but in a different outlet so as to rekindle their performance.

Meteoric advances in information technology and communications now create opportunities for work and employment that were not available to our parents and grandparents. In an earlier generation, the progression was clear and rigid: You went to college, obtained a professional degree, interviewed, and immediately went to work for a law firm, medical clinic, doctor's practice, engineering or architectural firm, or other business. In those days you probably worked all your life for that same firm or practice since lateral transfers were almost unheard-of.

The Changing Business Office

Now, however, instant communications and a mobile society mean you may change careers several times and may change employers dozens of times. In fact, many professional and technical temporary employees often work out of "alternative offices," which were pioneered by accounting firms in the late 1980s. With the use of computers, e-mail, laptops, ISDN lines, docking stations, cellular phones, and faxes, such workers can analyze, advise, and report without ever using a traditional office. Many companies increasingly provide offices for executives to store their records but expect them to be working outside that office and spending their time at clients' businesses or at the company's factories. Such alternative offices save large sums of leased-space money for companies and allow the employer to fit three to five executives into one traditional office.

Alternative offices are well suited for professional and technical temps who will not be concerned with territoriality and corporate political issues such as whose office is bigger or prettier or has the window view. These types of offices allow temporary employees especially to have greater flexibility and maximize their productivity for the employer. A recent survey by Hewlett-Packard Company documented that 99% of its alternative office users are satisfied and want its use expanded.

119

CHOOSING THE RIGHT STAFFING SERVICE

Personal Contacts

THE PEOPLE CLOSEST TO YOU, YOUR FAMILY AND FRIENDS, CAN BE very helpful. They may be able to answer your questions directly or, more importantly, put you in touch with someone else who can. This networking can lead to an "informational interview," where you can meet with someone who is willing to answer your questions about temporary staffing jobs and who can provide inside information. This is a highly effective way to learn the recommended type of training for certain positions, how someone in that position entered and advanced, and what he or she likes and dislikes about the work.

The Internet and Jobs

NEW GRADUATES AS WELL AS EMPLOYEES SEEKING LATERAL EMPLOY-ment moves have traditionally relied on networking, placement offices, headhunters, staffing services, and the employment classified newspaper advertisements in locating jobs. Now all these avenues are focused on the Internet. Certainly, the opportunities for networking are greatly enhanced by the chat rooms and talk groups as well as the information available on the Internet. Now many newspapers make their employment classified advertisements available on the Net, and many employers and recruiters advertise heavily on the Net. Web sites devoted to jobs include: The Riley Guide at http://www.jobtrak.com/ jobguide; America's Job Bank at http://www.ajb.dni.us; CareerMosaic at http://www.careermosaic.com; The Main Quad at http://develop. mainquad.com; The Monster Board at http://www.monster.com; and Online Career Center at http://www.occ.com. Government agencies also use the Net to post job openings. Staffing services now use the Net extensively.

Staffing services and the professional/technical employee benefit from the cost savings of the Internet. They avoid the postage costs of mailing resumes and applications. They defray the long distance telephone toll charges. And, they present themselves as up-to-date and modern by using the Internet.

Today, over 50% of companies surveyed by the American Management Association post job openings on the Internet and also use the Internet for recruiting and interviewing. The Internet ranked fourth in efficiency filling jobs behind newspaper advertising, trade publications, and personal referrals.

The growth of Web sites and on-line listings has made available a wide variety of resources at your fingertips if you have access to the Internet. Many public libraries offer access to the Internet if you do not have personal use of a computer at home. Staffing services, companies, professional societies, and government agencies maintain on-line resources or home pages, which are updated regularly with the latest information on their organization and its activities. Many of the Web sites for staffing services are listed in the Appendix.

Internet listings include such information as government documents, schedules of events, professional and technical job openings, classified employment ads, and even networking contacts. Listings for academic institutions provide links to career counseling and placement services through career resource centers, as well as information on financing your education. Colleges and universities also offer on-line guides to campus facilities for upgrades and refresher courses in your profession or area of expertise.

The various career information databases available through the Internet provide much of the same information available through libraries, career centers, and guidance offices. However, no single network or resource contains all desired information, so be prepared to search a number of different places for what you need. As in a library search, look through various lists by field or discipline, or by using particular keywords. It may even be helpful to consult a reference book such as *The Internet Yellow Pages*, which is available in most libraries.

Professional Societies, Trade Associations, Business Firms, and Educational Institutions

PROFESSIONAL AND EDUCATIONAL ORGANIZATIONS PROVIDE A VARIety of free or inexpensive career material. Consult the Internet or directories in your library's reference section for the names of staffing services. You may need to start with *The Guide to American Directories*, *The Directory of Directories*, or *The Internet Yellow Pages*. Another useful resource is *The Encyclopedia of Associations*, an annual multi-volume publication listing trade associations, professional societies, and fraternal and patriotic organizations.

The National Technical Information Service Center, a central source for all audiovisual material produced by the U.S. government, rents and sells material on jobs and careers. For a catalog, contact: National Technical Information Service Center, Springfield, VA 22161, phone 1-800-788-6282.

The National Association of Temporary Staffing Services has a Web site at http://www.natss.org.

Let's move on to the next chapter, which is about actually getting the appointment with the right service.

CHAPTER TEN

Getting to the Right Staffing Service

Sometimes It Takes More Than a Phone Call

MOST PEOPLE THINK GETTING AN APPOINTMENT WITH A SERvice is simply a matter of picking up the phone, dialing, and speaking with someone. It does involve that, but there are ways to do it and get the most results for your call (and earn the most money as a temp).

After you have done your research using referrals, reading the ads, and surfing the Internet, and have selected a staffing service, make your call. How friendly, professional, and helpful is the person answering the phone? Mondays are often the busiest days for services because of all of the recruiting ads they place in Sunday papers. Therefore, their phones may be busier than normal on Monday.

Know Whom to Ask For

KNOW WHOM TO ASK FOR WHEN YOU MAKE THAT FIRST CALL—HAVE A reason for calling.

Many services that use recruiting ads will list a person to ask for at the staffing service if the service is recruiting for a specific job. For instance, if a staffing service is trying to hire temps for an accounting firm, it may run an ad and tell you to ask for Rachel if you are interested in that job.

If you want that job, call that service and ask for Rachel. You will save a lot of time if you go directly to the person who is filling the specific job you want. If you do not talk to Rachel and you only want that specific job, you may waste time interviewing with other people in the staffing service who have jobs available you do not want. If you want accounting jobs, make sure you are talking to a representative who fills accounting jobs.

Jan was looking for a bookkeeping job. She did her research and reviewed the ads in the paper. She found several services that were advertising for bookkeeping jobs, some temp, some permanent.

Jan called in response to one ad that listed a temp-to-hire book-keeping job and asked to speak to Jim, the person listed in the staffing service's ad. She got an appointment with Jim at the staffing service the next day and was placed on the job she wanted that week. Jan did not waste her time talking to people who could not help her.

Tell the Staffing Service Why You Are Calling (You Need a Job)

IF YOU ARE NOT SURE WHAT TYPE OF TEMP JOB YOU WANT AND YOU JUST need to get to work and earn some money, investigate several Web sites or call several staffing services. Tell whoever answers your e-mail or the phone you want to fax your resume or come in and fill out a questionnaire or an application. If you want to make an appointment, ask when the first available appointment is. If the service tells you it is several days or weeks away, say you have an immediate need for money and you would like to come in and be worked in between appointments or you may have to go to another staffing service. Try to respond by sending your resume through the Internet or by fax. If that service does not seem to care or does not respond to your e-mail or fax, go somewhere else.

Some staffing services prefer to work by appointment only. That means they may schedule a phone appointment or interview in person. Others are open certain hours of the day to meet with potential temps. The smart and progressive staffing services know finding a good person is finding a good product, so they will try to work around your needs. If they do not, go somewhere else. Still others may require you to fax or fill out a questionnaire before they talk to you.

If you want to meet with a staffing service in person, some may see applicants Monday through Friday from the hours of 8:00 A.M. to 10:00 A.M. and 1:00 P.M. to 3:00 P.M. Others may interview people some evenings and weekends. If you have a professional technical skill that is in demand, a staffing service should be smart enough to work with your schedule. You should go where you think you can work in the jobs you like the most and can earn the most money.

When you go to a staffing service, make sure you apply with the right division. Many staffing services have several professional technical divisions. Do not go to accounting if you are an engineer.

How are you treated as a professional technical person? Are you asked to complete the same tests the clerical temp is taking? Not that there is anything wrong with being a clerical temp, but make sure you are using your time wisely. You can expect to fill out some of the same paperwork that all temps do, such as the required government paperwork, but you should not be expected to take the simple clerical and office tests that other temps take. If you are required to take them, you may have selected the wrong staffing service. If you are in an environment that seems like a cattle call, you may need to reconsider your choice. Appearances can be deceiving, but proceed with caution if you find yourself in this environment and do not expect much.

On the other hand, if you walk into what appears to be a tomb or funeral home type of environment, the staffing service may have too little activity to keep it in business. If you get a recording every time you call the office of a staffing service, you may be contacting a one-person shop. There is nothing wrong with one person running a staffing service; it just may take longer to talk to the one person in charge. There should be a happy medium. Activity, conversation among the staff, and a sense of purpose (i.e., finding you a job) are important. The staff should act like they expected you and they know what to do with someone with your skills. If they do not, go to another service.

Is the Staffing Service Qualified to Help You?

WHEN YOU HAVE SOMEONE FROM THE STAFFING SERVICE ON THE phone, try to qualify the types of positions the service has. Ask to speak to an interviewer, placement counselor, or staffing supervisor. (There are different titles used in the staffing industry for the person who will actually find you a job, so make sure you get to talk to the person who can help you the most.) Some services have staff who only interview or qualify people to be temps. These interviewers then refer the temps to the placement staff, who actually send or place temps on jobs. Other services have staff who both interview and place people on the job. It is important that you spend your time at a staffing service with the people who can help you, and that means getting to see the person who distributes the jobs you want.

When Mack walked into Brand X Staffing Service he was not sure exactly what he wanted to do. He had heard a lot of good things about Brand X from his friend Jean, who had temped for them evenings and weekends while she was in college. Mack arrived in the office of Brand X on Monday morning at 9:00 A.M. He'd had laboratory research experience in telemarketing and was looking for work to supplement his job as a musician in the evenings. He had a biology degree, but his choice of vocation was music and playing in a band.

Mack spoke with the receptionist, who asked him if he had an appointment. Mack admitted he did not have one. The receptionist then asked him if he was applying in response to an ad, and he said no.

The receptionist then made a phone call, and when she finished her call she told Mack that all of the placement staff were busy, but that he could complete an application and come back in two days for an interview. Mack completed the application and left.

He then went down the street two blocks to Superior Staffing Service. By then it was 11:00 A.M. The lobby was very busy. He didn't know much about Superior Staffing Service except that they advertised temporary and permanent scientific jobs in the classifieds.

The receptionist asked Mack if he had an appointment. He said no and the receptionist said no problem, someone would be with him soon. Another person from the service introduced himself to Mack and asked how he could help. Mack said he had an immediate need for income and wanted to do temp work. He went on to say he was especially interested in the laboratory research jobs the staffing service was recruiting for. The employee from Superior Staffing Service, Howard, reviewed the application with Mack, showed him how to complete it, and then reviewed the type jobs Superior Staffing had available. Mack worked for Superior Staffing almost a year six hours a day doing research and was named supervisor of the laboratory.

If you walk into a service with or without an appointment, give yourself plenty of time to complete the required government forms and possibly an application. A good rule is to allow at least two hours for every service you visit. Even if you have the skills most in demand, you will still be required to complete required paperwork by staffing services that conduct business in an ethical manner.

Allow yourself time to finish the application, take any required tests, and complete your interview. Do not schedule your appointments too close together in time; make sure that you will not be rushed going from one service to another. This includes phone interviews as well as in-person appointments.

CHAPTER ELEVEN

The Application Process

T HIS CHAPTER COVERS PROVIDING INFORMATION THROUGH THE Internet, completing all the paperwork, providing references and background information about yourself, and taking the tests. Interviewing is covered in Chapter 12.

Before you start filling out an actual application form, you may be asked to complete a form via the Internet. This information may be set up so that you will be filling in the blanks of what is actually a resume format. You could be asked whether you are an independent contractor, or a temporary employee about whom the staffing service you sign up with will be keeping W-2 information (see Chapter 2, "Staffing Services versus Headhunters versus Independent Contractors," for the difference between being a professional technical temp and being an independent contractor).

Kelly Services' Internet site has a Resume Maker that will allow you to fill in the blanks and send your resume to Kelly Services. The Net address is http://www.kellyservices.com. This format for resumes is an excellent guide to use for many professional technical jobs. The site allows you to submit or send the resume to Kelly Services.

When you actually talk to or meet with a staffing service representative, you may be asked to fill out an application so that the service will have information about you in a standard form that the service can easily computerize. If the staffing service has not entered your resume in a computerized system that can quickly be searched, the service will enter the application into such a system, which will allow your information to be pulled up by your name and by your skill. The service may also assign a number to your file, which could be your Social Security number.

The application for employment with a staffing service can consist of anywhere from 2 to 10 pages. In today's world you will be asked many things that your parents probably were not asked. For example, it is standard practice for most employers to ask a temp to consent to a background check and to take a drug test.

Background Checks

WHEN SOMEONE IS PAYING A STAFFING SERVICE TO FIND PEOPLE AND skills, the service wants to make sure people are who they say they are. Background checks will verify what you put on your application. An extensive background check will confirm where you grew up and where you went to high school, and also check what you are saying about college and advanced degrees. Your best bet is always to be truthful. If you did not complete college or graduate school, do not lie and say that you did. A background check will uncover this falsehood, and the staffing service will either fire you if you are already working for it or use the falsifying of information as a reason not to ever put you to work. Do not think because you are a professional technical temp you are beyond this type of check. A staffing service is paid for a product, and many services will invest in extensive background checks in order to keep honest people honest.

Many staffing services work with businesses that want a more extensive review. A criminal background check is an exploration of a person's background to see if there is any history of criminal activity. It can be done in the local court to see if a prospective temp has any outstanding warrants, has had an arrest, or has been convicted of a crime. Someone's record can also be checked on a statewide or national basis.

If the staffing service checks a prospective temp for criminal history, the service will do it by the person's birthday, Social Security number, current and past addresses, or driver's license number. Companies that specialize in background checks have become very sophisticated and are able to find out the facts. My advice would be to tell the service the truth about yourself. Sooner or later the truth will come out.

More and more businesses are conducting criminal record checks when hiring permanent employees and require the same investigations of temps who work on their premises. This is especially true for banks and financial institutions. Some banks have the same standards for temps who work for them as they do for their full-time employees. This means the temps would have to pass a criminal background check before they work there. The best rule is to always tell the truth.

Credit Checks

Background checks may also uncover your credit history. You have the right to ask exactly what the checks are that will be run on you. In fact, you would be smart to do so. It does not matter on every job what your credit history is. There are many people who find themselves in trouble with their creditors and the reason they have signed up with a staffing service is to straighten out or pay off their bills. The places where your credit history will matter are financial institutions. Places like banks or anyplace a temp is expected to handle money may try to avoid hiring someone who does not have an acceptable credit rating.

If you get turned down for a job with a staffing service because of your credit rating, do not despair. Not every single part-time or full-time temporary job requires that you pass a credit check. There are other jobs and plenty of staffing services that will gladly work with you. Paying off your debts is an honorable thing. You may ask to see your credit check or you can call your local credit bureau and for a nominal fee find out what exactly is being reported about you. Read on about what happened to Ashley with her credit check.

Ashley had been a full-time homemaker for the entire 20 years of her marriage. When she and her husband divorced she realized she would have to go to work outside the home. Ashley had studied library science in college and had volunteered with the public library system and archived books as well as helped with research. Ashley decided to register with a staffing service that could help her use these skills to find work.

The staffing service had a bank as a client, and this particular bank needed a temp to catalog all its records. The skills Ashley had picked up as a volunteer for the library made her a good candidate for the job. The staffing service had Ashley sign a consent form that would allow the service to conduct a routine credit and criminal background check; this was a requirement for any temp to work in this particular bank.

Imagine Ashley's surprise when the credit check reported her ex-husband was not paying bills. Even though he and Ashley were divorced, Ashley's credit rating was affected by bills that had both of their names on them. Fortunately for Ashley, the scores on this credit rating still allowed her to work at this bank, but the experience was a rude awakening for her as to what type of credit she really had as a result of her ex-husband's activities.

If you have a question about your credit rating, call your local credit bureau. It should be able to provide you with the same record that it will release to a staffing service about your credit rating.

Some businesses require a certain credit rating before a temp can work for them. These businesses are usually banks that have credit standards for their full-time employees and want to apply the same standards to temps. Remember, while a bad credit rating will prevent you from working in some businesses, others will not care. The reason you are temping is to make money.

Drug Tests

OF COURSE, MOST WORK ENVIRONMENTS ARE DRUG-FREE. THAT brings up drug testing. If you are not willing to take a drug test, be prepared to have a hard time finding a job. If you say no to a test, it will look like you have something to hide. As a temp, you may have to take a drug test before the staffing service ever puts you to work or you may have to take a drug test when you actually go to work. Make sure you list all medications you are taking when you take the test; this includes aspirin and vitamins. Good drug tests will turn up anything legal as well as illegal that you are taking.

Staffing services will ask you to submit to a drug test again if you are ever hurt on the job. This is to make sure you were not under the influence of anything like alcohol, marijuana, or cocaine while you were working. You might also have to agree to random drug testing as part of the requirement of working for a staffing service or at the request of the company where you are sent as a temp. Companies entrust valuable equipment and computers to professional and technical temps, so they do not want someone who is not sober.

Drug testing is usually done by testing a urine sample for substances like alcohol, marijuana, cocaine, and prescription medicine. It is illegal to use some of these drugs, and people can be fired for being under the influence of drugs. As a result, many companies have random drug testing of their employees or they test employees without warning them to see if they are using drugs. Someone who tests positive for an illegal drug can be fired.

If a temp tests positive for drugs, a service can choose not to work them. Many services will not even let you sign up for temp work unless you agree to be tested for drugs.

Services may test temps on-site or send them to laboratories to give a urine sample to be tested for drugs. Many prescriptions and over-the-counter drugs will show up in these tests, so always list any recent medications you have taken when taking a drug test.

Jeremy was excited about the job as a computer analyst a staffing service found for him. If all went well, he would work as a temp for the staffing service, and then after three months become a permanent employee of a research firm. One of the requirements for starting the temp job was taking a drug test. Jeremy had a cold and had been taking medicine prescribed by his doctor. When he arrived at the designated lab to take the test he was asked to list all medications he was taking. Jeremy did not list the medicine for his cold because it was legal and he did not think it mattered.

Imagine his surprise when the staffing service called and said he would not be able to start the temp-to-hire job because he flunked the drug test. Jeremy was pretty much a straight-arrow type of guy, so he was stunned. The staffing service told him what he tested positive for, and Jeremy was able to verify it was a prescribed medicine he was on. He had to take the test again and was finally able to start the job. But, he could have lost the position to another candidate due to the delay, and he was lucky he did not. He could have avoided the risk had he listed the medication as he was requested to do the first time he took the test.

I-9 Forms (or Proof of Eligibility to Work)

OTHER PREAPPLICATION QUESTIONS WILL ASK YOU TO PROVE THAT you are eligible to work. In the United States a law was passed in the 1980s requiring businesses to make sure their staff are legal residents so as to be eligible to work. As a result, businesses that hire workers, including the temporary staffing industry, now require all workers to have proof of eligibility to work. A passport meets this requirement, or two forms of identification, one with a photograph, such as a photo driver's license.

As part of this process, you must complete an I-9 form before you are given an application. The I-9 document has a place for your name, address, and Social Security number. The service will complete a section listing your forms of identification. Bring a passport if you have one, or some other type of identification with a photo. The service may accept a driver's license that has a photo plus either a copy of your birth certificate or your Social Security card.

If you refuse to do either drug testing or an I-9 form, you probably will not be allowed to apply for temp work with the staffing service. The reasons that staffing services are so strict are that the temporary employment can be reviewed by the government at any time for failure to comply with the legal requirement of an I-9, and many employers want assurance from the staffing service that the temps are drug-free.

When Lorie made an appointment with a staffing service she was very excited. The service had already reviewed her resume and felt she was qualified for several current job openings the service was trying to fill. When the service told Lorie she would need to bring in proof of her eligibility to work, Lorie only half listened to their instructions.

Lorie showed up for her appointment and when she started to complete her I-9 form with its proof of eligibility requirement she told the service she had only her driver's license with her. The staffing service was adamant and insisted Lorie provide the other required ID before any talk about putting her to work. She then went to the nearest Social Security office and requested a card. The moral of the story is, be prepared. If you do not have the forms of ID needed, order them before you start your job search. It will save you time and help you earn money sooner. It may take at least six weeks from the time you apply before you receive a Social Security card.

The Application

THE APPLICATION ITSELF CAN BE LENGTHY (UP TO 10 PAGES) EVEN IF a staffing service already has your resume. Again, this is to comply with government regulations. The application can include extensive sections on your education, work history, the types of skills you have, and the scores for any tests you might take, as well as an analysis of your appearance and personality and a place for references. This chapter addresses the application by section, much like many employment service applications are divided by section.

The application will include spaces for your name, address, Social Security number, phone number, and who is to be contacted in case of emergency. The rest is pretty standard and is likely to include the following:

Education

THERE WILL BE A SECTION FOR YOUR EDUCATION THAT INCLUDES high school, technical, college, or any advanced degrees you have. Be accurate on your education, because more and more correspondence is sent and phone calls are made by prospective employers, including services, to verify that what you have listed for your education is true.

Tim listed on his application that he had a B.S. from the University of California. The service he applied with did a background check on Tim's education and found he was eight hours short of a degree. As a result, Tim was fired from the staffing service for falsifying his records.

Work History

STAFFING SERVICES WANT TO KNOW THE TYPE OF JOB EXPERIENCE anyone wanting to temp has had, so they can better match the current skills of the temp to the job market. Services may ask you to list your employment history for many years or just through the past couple of years. Every staffing service is different.

What staffing services may ask you in the work history section of the application is where you worked, when you worked there, what your title was, what your job responsibilities were, who your supervisor was, the reason you left that job, and what the phone number is there. The reasons for these questions are to match you to the most appropriate temp job and to be able to have a reference to check.

Amy had been a paralegal for a law firm in Chicago. When she went to register for temp work she listed the years she had worked there (1988–1996), her title as a paralegal, what her responsibilities were, her reason for leaving or layoff, her supervisor's name, and his phone number.

The service where she registered asked that temps complete their work history for as long as they had been in the workforce. Amy had been working for almost 20 years, so she continued listing her work history. Her most recent job had been with the law firm. Before that she had worked as a researcher for a national information technology company for eight years on a part-time basis. She could not remember her supervisor's name, so she gave the service the name of the personnel officer. She then gave the name of another company where she had worked years previously.

The service could tell that Amy had office experience from the law firm and some research experience before that. The main thing to remember when completing the work history section is to be as accurate as possible. Services are interested in what you have done, and you also want to make sure you tell the truth about yourself. The reason for that is the staffing services may use your work history as part of checking your references.

Some staffing services will take resumes as a summary of a temp's work history. Other services will ask anyone completing an application to complete the work history section of the application and will file a resume with it.

References

ONE OF THE REASONS BUSINESSES USE STAFFING SERVICES IS TO HAVE qualified people working in their offices. Staffing services have become more aggressive in checking out people's background because many businesses do not want to take the time to check references on their staff, so they rely on the staffing service to do so. That is why some staffing services will pay an outside source to check out a prospective temp and will ask that the check include criminal, education, and reference checks. Other services will conduct their own reference checks, usually calling those listed as references on a prospective temp's application or by contacting the references listed on resumes submitted by the professional technical temp.

The service where Amy applied called her supervising attorney at the law firm to get a reference on Amy. Many businesses will only verify dates of employment of its former employees. Some will say whether an employee is eligible for rehire and what type of employee that person was when he or she worked there.

Some staffing services may ask temps to complete a written request for a reference check, and the service will mail that form with the former employee's signature on it to the former employer asking for a reference. Other services do all of their reference checks by phone. Be prepared to give references when you apply to a staffing service. If you have any written letters of recommendation, take copies with you to leave with the staffing service.

When the staffing service called the supervising attorney about Amy, he told them it was the policy of the law firm to only give out the dates of employment of its former employees on the phone. He said Amy worked for them from 1988 to 1996. He did say he would comply with a written request for a reference from the service if they mailed it to him.

Amy had also obtained the permission of her adviser and a former teacher to use them as references, and listed them on her application. If you have limited work history, ask someone you know to be a personal reference. People at schools and organizations where you may have done volunteer work are good choices.

Sarah, on the other hand, did not tell the truth on her application and got caught. She listed that she worked for a major telecommunications company in San Francisco from 1991 to 1996 as a technical writer. When the staffing service called to check her work history, it was told the company could only give out dates of employment. The company said Sarah worked from 1992 to 1995. When the staffing service called Sarah to check on the dates, she admitted she had wanted to look like she had more experience than she really did have, since the job she wanted listed five years' experience as a requirement. The staffing service would not offer Sarah a job because she lied about her dates of employment and falsified her application.

Testing

SERVICES CAN TEST PEOPLE FOR BOTH GENERAL AND SPECIFIC SKILLS. The service wants to impress the businesses that order temps from them, so they test the people who want to temp for them. That way the service has proof that a temp is qualified to do what the businesses request the temp to do. The better the temp does, the better the service does, and the more business it will get. Staffing services are in the employment business to make money, and they want to send out a product, or temp, who will make them the most money and who will do the best job.

Specific tests should cover your area of professional or technical expertise and might include accounting, engineering, medical, or legal terminology and computer skills. When a hospital calls a staffing service and requests someone to supervise a medical practice, the hospital wants a temp who knows medical terminology. The staffing service will often want to test someone who claims to have this knowledge. By testing the temp, the service will find out whether the person is really qualified to do the job.

Most specific testing by staffing services today involves the computer. When engineer John applied with a staffing service, he described on his application the various computer programs and software packages with which he was experienced. By testing John on the specific software he had worked on, the service was able to qualify him for various types of temp positions.

John had also checked on his application that he could use financial spreadsheets on Lotus, so he was tested for that as well. That meant John was able to work more temp jobs with accounting firms and healthcare companies and make more money.

Rebecca was a temp that Service XYZ sent to a bank in Seattle to help organize and supervise the training program. Rebecca had a college degree in counseling and had developed strong organizational skills raising her children and coordinating all the activities in her home. She had also organized several events for her favorite charity. Rebecca used this knowledge and experience plus her people skills to get the bank's training program functioning smoothly. She developed a system that the bank was able to continue to use after she finished her assignment.

The Contract

MANY STAFFING SERVICES REQUEST EVERYONE WHO COMPLETES AN application to sign a contract with them. Read the contract carefully. Many of them say you will not accept a permanent job that you found as a result of being a temporary without notifying the staffing service. This means whoever offers you a job may have to pay the staffing service a fee to hire you. This fee probably will be paid up front by the business to the staffing service.

Or, the business and the staffing service may agree to work you through the payroll of the staffing service for so many hours until the business has paid the service for you. For example, you may have been on a temp assignment at a company for two weeks when the company offers you a permanent job. You consult with the staffing service that sent you there. The company and staffing service agree that you will work as a temp through the staffing service for eight more weeks and the business will be in effect paying a fee for you by the hour instead of in one lump sum. At the end of the eight weeks the staffing service will have made a profit and the company will be free to hire you.

Staffing services are in business to make money. Most will charge the business where they place you an hourly fee for using them. If the contract of the staffing service ever charges you, the temp, do not work with that service.

Again, be sure to read the contract carefully. Ask for a copy if you need to, and understand what you are signing. If a staffing service is smart, it will work with you if you are ever offered a full-time job as a result of being a temp for the service. Temps who are placed or hired by customers of the staffing service are walking testimonials about what a good job the staffing service does in recruiting qualified people to temp for it.

Don started temping for Shady Staffing Service when his division was downsized. He'd been surprised to find himself among the downsized as he had always been a loyal employee, and when starting work at his former employer, a bank, right out of college, he thought he would be there for several years. The bank was one of the largest banks in his state and did so well that it was acquired by a large regional bank.

The large regional bank that acquired Don's bank already had many accountants, so they let Don go. Don panicked, did no research, and signed up with Shady Staffing Service, the first staffing service he could find that placed experienced accountants on temp-to-hire jobs.

Don did not read the contract Shady Staffing Service required all of its professional technical temps to sign. Shady Staffing Service sent Don out on a job that was temp-to-perm, meaning Don would work as a temp for three months, then become a full-time employee of the business where he temped. Don did not interview or preview the job; he just started work there one day.

It turned out that Don was working in an office that was a front for people who ran the numbers or gambled illegally in his city. He did not like the job, and told Shady Staffing Service he did not want to stay. Shady told him he would have to work there a year or pay Shady Staffing, as required by the contract, 10% of his first year's salary as a penalty for not staying on the job. Don paid Shady the 10% penalty because he was afraid not to.

The moral of this story is never to work for a staffing service that will charge you any money—either finder's fee or penalty. There are too many services that will not charge you money, so why bother with the ones who do?

Don made two mistakes. First, he did not research the staffing service where he wanted to work. No one Don knew had ever worked for Shady Staffing Service, and he made no attempt to investigate it. The second mistake was that he did not read carefully what he signed. If you, as a professional technical temp, ever feel that a staffing service is pressuring you into signing something you do not understand, leave. Or, If you still want to work for this service, it's worth the time and expense to have an attorney read the contract and advise you about what you are to sign.

Don, hopefully, learned his lesson and in the future will only work for those staffing services that have a good reputation. Stay away from the ones like Shady!

CHAPTER TWELVE

The Interview

(Or, How to Get the Person You Talk with to Give You the Best Jobs— First Impressions Really Do Count!)

The People You Meet Will Find You Good Jobs or Bad Jobs

A S YOU START YOUR PROCESS OF BECOMING A PROFESSIONAL technical temp you will probably have contact with a staffing service through the Internet and by phone. Once you get to the application stage, you will be interviewed in person by someone at the service. It is important that you conduct yourself in a professional manner from the very first time you make contact with the staffing service by e-mail to in-person communication. You want to establish a good working relationship with everyone you meet at the service, because they will know before you do what temp jobs are available. The nicer you are to them, the better your chances are of getting the best temp jobs. This goes for everyone you meet at the service, from the receptionist to the interviewer to the placement counselor to the bookkeeper.

Be Nice to the Receptionist

A CRUCIAL RULE TO REMEMBER IS ALWAYS TO BE NICE TO THE RECEP-tionist. That person who answers the phone or greets you at the front door could very well be the person who has read and edited your e-mail for the placement office. Some staffing services are so small that the receptionist is part of the staff who will interview you and make the decision whether to place you on a job.

Consider what happened to Joyce. She went to We Care Staffing Service to get a professional technical temp job. We Care Staffing was a small company, and the staff took turns covering the front desk each day so that the receptionist could go to lunch. Joyce came in for an appointment at 11:30 A.M. at We Care Staffing Service, and the person covering the front desk was trying to answer three phone lines, all ringing.

Joyce was very rude to the person at the front desk as she started to complete her application. The full-time receptionist came back from lunch. The person who had originally greeted Joyce, and to whom she had been so rude, turned out to be the person who was responsible for placing her on high-paying professional technical temporary jobs.

The first impression Joyce made with We Care Staffing was that the service would always have to counsel her on her manners when it sent her out on temp jobs. As a result, she missed out on several high-paying temp jobs from We Care Staffing Service, because no one wanted to risk sending her to a job where her bad manners could cost the service a client. If only Joyce had taken the time to be pleasant to the "receptionist," her manners would not have been cause for concern.

Another reason to be nice to the receptionist, other than that it is just plain common sense and good manners, is that the placement staff of the service may ask the receptionist for his or her impression of you. When I placed people on jobs, I often asked the receptionist for an impression of the person I was trying to place. I did not try very hard to help a person who was not nice to the receptionist. Rude behavior is never acceptable; good manners will help you get the job you want. Oftentimes you may be on the phone with the receptionist first, and later you may be alone in the lobby with that person, who will have time to form an opinion of you. The next time the receptionist calls the interviewer or person who can offer you temp jobs, the interviewer may ask the receptionist on the phone what impression has been formed of you so far. This is a common practice in the staffing industry.

The receptionist could turn out to be a very important ally for you. The receptionist can tell you what the best temp jobs are and how to make a good impression with the rest of the service staff. The receptionist may also make sure your phone calls to the service go to the person who can help you get the job you want and in which you will make the most money.

It is important to make a good impression, because this person can either make or break you in the temporary world. The first impression that you make with this person can have a lasting effect on your success as a temp.

Make the Right Impression with Your Wardrobe

HERE ARE SOME SUGGESTIONS THAT WILL HELP YOU MAKE THE RIGHT impression:

Dress professionally. This interview should be just as important as an interview for any permanent job. If you want to work in an office and you are a man, wear a jacket and slacks or a suit, a dress shirt, and a tie. If you are a woman, wear a suit, a tailored pantsuit, or a dress (do not wear a miniskirt). Make sure your clothes look like they have been pressed.

Avoid flashy jewelry or accessories. Do not wear too much jewelry or makeup. A good rule is to be understated in your appearance rather than overstated.

Look the interviewer in the eye, be pleasant, and have a firm handshake. Avoid strong cologne, aftershave, or perfume. Use a mouthwash or have a mint to eat before you interview. Never chew gum at the service while you are completing the application, testing, or being interviewed on the phone or in person.

The person who interviews will give you a grade on your appearance and personality as well as your skills. In fact, many staffing services have codes that allow the interviewer to immediately select an impression of what type of environment you seem most suited for. This impression comes as much from the way you dress and communicate as from what skills you have to offer.

Try to dress as you would if you were going to an interview for a full-time job. Even if you do not have a lot of money to spend on clothes, you can still be neat and clean.

If you are not dressed in a way that is appropriate for the professional technical temporary work you are applying for, someone from the staffing service may offer constructive criticism about your appearance. Do not be offended. The staffing service is just trying to set you up for a win-win situation. It is important to the staffing service that you succeed. If you do not succeed, the service does not make money, so listen to any suggestions about dress.

If you do not dress appropriately or conduct yourself professionally, the service could document this on your application or on your record. The service may avoid sending you to their best clients. This will affect the amount of money you can make as a temp.

You don't have to have a lot of money to dress nicely and to be clean. You may be placed in an office environment that has a casual dress code. More and more businesses are being flexible about their dress code. The service should advise you about dress codes where they place you.

Be pleasant and professional with your service interviewer. Use correct grammar and mind your manners. No one wants to send out a temp who is rude and will not be a good representative of the service. Remember: You, the temp, are the product that the service sells. In order for the service to make money, you have to do a good job and make them look good in the eyes of the public.

When Jessica went to Service A she was nervous, since it was the first time she had ever tried temp work. She had a few years' work experience, found herself between jobs, and did not know what she wanted to do next; she just knew she had to have an income while she looked.

She wanted to work temp as an office manager in the Dallas area, so she dressed for her interview at the temp service as if she were an employee of the type of company she wished to temp for. She wore a navy business suit, plain navy pumps, a white shirt, and pearls. She avoided any heavy perfume. She even checked her teeth in the mirror of her car before she went into the service to make sure she had no food particles in her mouth.

Jessica made a very good first impression with her interviewer and was offered a temp job starting the next day. She did not always have to dress as conservatively as she did on the day she interviewed with the service, but that good first impression she made with the interviewer went a long way in landing her well-paying temp jobs while she worked for the service.

Jared, on the other hand, did not try to make a good impression. He was an excellent engineer in the defense industry in southern California, but a little deficient in people skills. He figured it did not matter how he looked when he went to meet the service staff, since he would not really be working there. He thought it only mattered how he looked when he went out to different places to temp.

Jared did not take a bath or shower on the day of his interview with the service. Instead, he splashed on some strong aftershave. He put on some khakis he had worn the previous day that were not pressed, a casual shirt, and loafers with no socks. He did shave but forgot to brush his teeth. He decided to chew gum instead of brushing or using mouthwash. He also wore his biggest earring, a bracelet, and matching necklace.

Jared did not bother to shake hands with the interviewer, did not have good eye contact, slouched in his chair, and chewed gum the whole time of his interview. The interviewer told him he thought Jared had great engineering skills but that he would need guidance on how to dress before he could be placed on any jobs. (The good staffing services will tell a temp that, so the temp will not be set up for failure by his or her appearance.)

Jared was very embarrassed when he realized the service thought he did not know how to dress for work or the importance of being clean. He told the interviewer he had not thought it mattered how he looked when he met with the service, that it only mattered how he looked when he worked for them. He could have saved himself a lot of embarrassment by preparing appropriately.

The story does have a happy ending. Jared finished his interview and acted in a professional manner the rest of the time he was with the staffing service. He went home, cleaned up, changed his clothes, and returned to the service, where he asked to speak to the person who had previously interviewed him. Jared was able to assure the service he would be a good representative and knew how to present himself. He was then placed by the staffing service on engineering jobs that paid very well. He was even able to wear a knit shirt, khakis, and tennis shoes to most of his jobs.

Match Your Skills and Background to Temp Jobs Available

AFTER YOU HAVE GOTTEN THROUGH THE FIRST-IMPRESSION STAGE OF your interview, concentrate on matching your skills to the jobs you will enjoy and in which you will make the most money. The person who interviews you may be the person who places you on the job or may introduce or refer you to the person in the service who does that.

What the interviewer will do is review your application. You will be asked about your job history. Be prepared to say what you liked and disliked about previous jobs. For example, if you like working in a fast-paced environment, tell the interviewer that. If you hate answering phones, share that also. If you like figuring out how to use various computer programs, say so. What you do not want to happen is to be placed in an environment where you cannot be productive. The interview should be the place to address your preferences.

The interview should cover areas like how proficient you are with computers and whether you have any accounting or bookkeeping skills. Every temporary job is different, and it is the duty of the interviewer to determine where you fit in.

Other Suggestions for Interviewing

THE BOOK *POWER INTERVIEWS: JOB-WINNING TACTICS FROM FORTUNE 500 Recruiters*, by Neil Yeager and Lee Hough, published by John Wiley & Sons, revised and expanded in 1998, offers the following suggestions.

Practice interviewing in the car, in front of the mirror, and with friends. Learn as much as you can about the employer you will be working for (in this case the staffing service, and later the company where the staffing service places you). There are practical questions you can use in any interview, such as asking why the job is available. Is it a new position created by growth, or is it available because someone was promoted or terminated? Was the temp in the job before you hired by the company, or did the temp quit the assignment because of working conditions?

There are two commonly asked questions that come up in most interviews, and Yeager and Hough offer answers to both. The first is, "Why do you feel you can be successful in this position?" The winner answer is, "Given my history, this is the perfect position at this point in my career. I have been studying this field and watching your organization for several years in anticipation of such an opportunity. I have the requisite skills [tell a brief story to prove it]. I am in a perfect position to take this job and really run with it."

The other frequently asked question is, "What are your greatest strength and weakness, and how will these affect your performance here?" The winner answer from Yeager and Hough is, "In terms of strengths, I believe my greatest asset is that I have a highly organized mind, capable of creating order out of confusion. My greatest weakness perhaps is that I have little patience for people who don't value the same sense of order that I do. I believe my organizational skills can help this organization achieve its goals more quickly, and that my appreciation for streamlining complex problems can sometimes rub off on my coworkers."

The bottom line is that a staffing service is trying to find out how you can make them money. The staffing service has already sold a business on how that business will make money by using the staffing service; now it is up to you to sell yourself as the right person for the job, whether it be a short-term temp job, a temp-to-hire job, or a long-term working relationship with a staffing service.

Yeager and Hough suggest keeping in mind the popular term "value added," which means everyone in a company will be able to "demonstrate in very specific terms the impact of his or her contribution to the strength and prosperity of the organization." Or, "that each player makes a clear measurable contribution" at one's place of work. In your answers in the interview process, keep thinking of what you bring to the table, what you add to the company, and what skills you offer.

It is not always skills that will cause a staffing service to select you. In fact, Paul Sharps of Global Dynamics, an information technology staffing service in California, says attitude and aptitude go hand in hand. A willingness to learn and the right attitude are often the deciding factors when a service selects a candidate for the job. That does not mean you should have a phony personality, but you should make the effort to be polite and get along with someone. Take the story of what happened to Fran and Bea.

Fran and Bea were both candidates for a job through an information technology staffing service. Both of them contacted the service through the Internet, and both had great resumes. The recruiter from the staffing service set up a time via e-mail to do a phone interview with each of them to see who would be the better candidate for a 12-month assignment that paid $122,000.

When the recruiter from the service spoke with Fran, she was very abrupt. As the recruiter tried to verify Fran's skills and the type of salary she needed, Fran answered the questions in a condescending and sarcastic manner. There was no need for her to be rude to the recruiter. The recruiter was just doing a job, but Fran acted superior to the recruiter, who she believed was stupid and unimportant.

What Fran did not know was the recruiter was very important, because the recruiter was the first person in the staffing service structure who needed to be convinced the applicant would make a good information technology temp for the service. Then the recruiter would need to sell or convince the supervisor or account manager, who would screen the temp again before setting her up for a job with a client.

When the same recruiter called Bea, the recruiter could tell she was nervous, because she spoke rapidly. Bea even admitted she was nervous, but she also said she really wanted the job and asked the recruiter what advice the recruiter had for her. The recruiter told Bea to relax and take a deep breath and be herself.

When the recruiter met with the account manager to discuss hiring Fran or Bea, the recruiter said Fran had more programs and skills listed that would qualify her for the job, but the recruiter also hesitated when recommending Fran. The account manager asked why there was hesitation, and the recruiter said the service would probably have to spend a lot of time coaching Fran on her people skills in order to work with the client. The recruiter went on to say Bea had fewer programming skills but a better attitude. As a result, the account manager for the staffing service chose Bea as the candidate to be presented to the client, because people skills were a deciding factor when sending temps to this particular client. As a result, because Bea took the time to be polite, she received a better-paying job than Fran simply because the staffing service people liked her better.

The moral of this story is, manners count. Fran could have been insecure or just having a bad day. Some people who find themselves entering the world of temporary employment do not have good self-esteem. They may view themselves as failures when they are not. If they view themselves as failures, they may have a tendency to be hateful to others who are trying to help them. If you are having one of those hours or one of those days, watch the tone of your voice and the way you communicate with others. Being nice is never the wrong thing to do when talking with a staffing service.

Tell Them the Hours, Days, Weeks, Months, and Even Years You Want to Work

YOU WILL BE ASKED WHEN YOU CAN START WORK. SOME SERVICES WILL send you to a temp job the very day you sign up with them. You will be asked what hours you can work. For example, do you want to work days, evenings, weekends, every day, half days, or a few days a week? You can expect to be given a choice of the length of time you want to work. Do you want to go to the same job for five days in a row, six weeks in a row, or for several months or even years? Or, do you like variety and want to change jobs every few days?

The world of professional technical temping is both similar to and different from traditional office temping. You will make more because of your skills, and your job assignments may be longer. There could be some days when you are called in the morning and asked to go to work that day. Or, you may be given a week's notice of when you will start work. The point is, you need to share with the staffing service what your preferences are. If you want to work every day, tell the service that.

Many people work temp because of the flexibility of work. That means you are choosing a lifestyle outside of the traditional nine-to-five world. Many professional technical temps would rather work a 60-hour week one week, then have the next two weeks off. You are the only person who knows what works best for you. You must make sure you are communicating effectively with the service you work with to make sure you are offered jobs that fit with your lifestyle and budget.

Find Out What Temp Jobs Are Available

AS YOUR APPLICATION IS REVIEWED, THE INTERVIEWER MAY SHARE information about the businesses where the staffing service places temps. They may ask you if you want to work in a healthcare company, a hospital, a bank, the entertainment industry, a big corporation, or a small business.

Do you know the type of environment you want to work in? The wonderful thing about temping is it allows you flexibility. Even if you left a conservative, regimented environment, you may be looking at temping as a way to get back into that type of work structure. You could also be looking for temp work to get into a different type of environment.

Marion was a paralegal who worked for a big law firm where there were more than 200 lawyers. She spent 10 years working for two contract lawyers in the firm. That firm lost four of their biggest clients one year, and the firm decided to restructure; Marion lost her job. She used her severance package to pay off her credit card bills, and decided she would go through a staffing service to find her next job. When the service asked her what type of job she wanted, she said she wanted to work in a law firm that was less structured than her previous employer.

The service sent Marion to a job that started the next week. It was an indefinite job assignment, which meant the service did not know how long the job would last. The law firm had two defense attorneys who had accepted a heavily publicized criminal law case, and they needed a great deal of criminal investigative research done and done quickly. Marion was able to use her research skills, and she found she enjoyed the pace of criminal work more than corporate contracts. She went on to a permanent job at another law firm as a result of the excellent references she received from the two defense attorneys for whom she temped.

The More You Call the Staffing Service the More You Will Work

FIND OUT WHICH INDIVIDUAL IN THE STAFFING SERVICE YOU NEED TO call to be placed in the jobs you want. Take that person's business card with you. Some services will tell you to call every day that you are available to work unless the service already has you on the job.

The more often you call and communicate with the service, the more you will work and the more money you will make. You cannot call a service too often. Remember, the service probably has hundreds of other people who temp for them. The person who calls the service the most will be on the service's mind the most and will be called back the most for jobs. If you do not call the service, the service will forget about you and may call someone else first for work.

If you do not stay in contact with a service, your file will be deleted or your resume shredded after a period of time. If you have a skill that is in demand and you tell a service you will be available in three days, weeks, or months, the service will note that in your file, usually in a computer, and call you back around the time you said you would be available for work. That is because the service knows it can make money from your skills and wants you to go to work for it instead of another service.

Bob applied for work with Service ABC on a Monday morning. He told the staffing service he needed to start work that week. Karen, the person who interviewed Bob, told him she would be the person from the service who would place him on temp jobs.

Karen and Bob reviewed his background and qualifications as an accountant, and Karen administered some computer tests for Bob to see what jobs would be best for him. He did very well, so Karen said she would look for a position that would use his skills and that was in his pay range.

Karen told Bob she placed a lot of accountants on temp jobs every week in the city. Bob had chosen this particular staffing service because the service had a good reputation and a lot of good clients. Karen also told Bob that she called the people first for temp jobs who called her and told her they wanted to work. Karen said the more often Bob called her, the more he would work. Karen closed the interview by saying that at the moment she had her positions filled for that week, but Bob could call her that afternoon or the next morning if he was still available to work temp.

Bob called Karen late Monday afternoon, and she offered him a job that used his accounting background, started the next day, and would last for two weeks. Bob got the job because he was persistent. As long as he worked for that service, Karen gave him good jobs because he continued to call her frequently.

Your Paycheck—Know How to Get It!

FIND OUT WHAT YOU HAVE TO DO TO GET PAID. MOST SERVICES WILL give you a time slip or time card to use as a form of documentation of your hours or project work.

The service should explain to you how to complete the record of work. Many time cards have a place for your name and your Social Security number and list the days of the week. You will be responsible for filling in the blank spaces. You might need to fill in the dates as well as the hours you work each day of the week. Most businesses where you temp will keep a copy of the time card you complete while working at that business. The service should tell you who from the business where you are working will sign your time card, but if not, you need to find out from the place where you are working who is to verify your hours. This is important; if you do not get this handled right at the start of your assignment, it could delay your getting paid in a timely manner.

The service should tell you how to process your time slip, and how often you will be paid. Staffing services vary; you may be paid weekly, twice a month, or monthly. The service will tell you when the deadline is for turning in your time card. You can probably fax in the time card. On rare occasions, it may have to be mailed or dropped off in person. Some services have representatives who will pick up the time card and take it to the service for you. You need to know what you are responsible for when it comes to your time card.

Make sure you get your time card in on time. If you do not, you may not get paid on payday. The service has the right to wait and pay you in the next pay period if you do not follow procedures. For example, if a staffing service pays on Friday, it may tell temps to have their time cards turned in by the end of the day on Tuesday. Every service is different.

Most services will make the temps accountable for completing the time card. If a temp turns in an incomplete time card, the service may refuse to pay or delay paying the temp for not following instructions and completing the time card. Look what happened to Elizabeth in New Orleans.

Elizabeth went to her first temp job at an insurance company as a technical writer. The staffing service had given her instructions on how to complete her time card and the deadline for turning it in. The service paid its temps on Fridays and needed to receive time cards by Wednesday at 8:00 A.M.

Elizabeth mailed her time card to the service Tuesday night at 10:00 P.M. The time card arrived at the service on Thursday. When Elizabeth went to the service on Friday to pick up her paycheck, it was not there. That was because she had not followed the directions of the staffing service regarding when to turn in her record of work in order to be paid on a regular basis.

Most people are working as professional technical temps as a way to make money. Make sure you get all the money you have earned; keep good records. The best records are copies of the time cards that you complete for the service. They provide a written record of the hours you have worked should you or the service ever have a disagreement about the hours you should be paid.

CHAPTER THIRTEEN

Accepting Your First Temp Job

(Get All of the Facts)

FINALLY, THE REASON YOU ARE HERE IS TO GET A JOB SO YOU CAN make money. You have gone through all of the paperwork, given your references, taken the tests, and had your interview, and you may have surfed the Net and perused every Web site of your profession. Now the service is prepared to offer you a job. Should you take it?

You may be offered your first temp job on the day you fax your resume, or you may go in and fill out your application and then be called at home by the service several days, weeks, or months from the day you came in and asked for work. Every service is different. How soon you receive an assignment will depend on how flexible you are with salary, travel, and the hours you work and how marketable your skills are.

How flexible are you on your salary? Do you want $30 an hour but will accept $20 to get some immediate income? The amount of money you will accept per hour is something only you can decide.

Urgency is another factor that may have some bearing on when you go to work. If you really need immediate income, tell the service you are ready to work that day, and ask the placement person to find you something. A sense of urgency can often help you get work faster.

Why You Are on the Temp Job: The Business Calls the Staffing Service

THERE ARE TWO WAYS STAFFING SERVICES GET TEMP JOBS TO OFFER you.

One way is by having businesses call them when they need a temp and tell them what job they need the temp to perform. For example, a drugstore may call a service and say a temp is needed to come in and assist as a pharmacist that day, as one of the regular pharmacists is out sick. The service should find out what the licensing requirements are as well as the professional tasks a temp may need to perform, like filling prescriptions or communicating with doctors or insurance companies. The service will then send a qualified temp in who can work that day. Ideally, the service will already have several pharmacists registered with it and know who is available to work immediately.

Is someone out sick? Is there a job vacancy? Is this a special project? In other words, why did the business call the service for a temp? Find out why the business called in a temp order. This is really important if you are temping to find a permanent job. In that case, you will want to focus on the temp jobs that are available as a result of a job vacancy.

If someone is out sick, you could be on that job for any number of days. You could fill in for someone who is sick one day if it is a minor illness, a week if it is the flu, or six to eight weeks if the worker has had surgery.

Nora was sent to a business by Selective Staffing Service in Pittsburgh to be a semiconductor process and equipment engineer. The business where she was placed had asked the service to send someone who could start work that day and fill in for the business's full-time engineer, who was sick. The business did not know how long the engineer would be out sick.

Nora reported to work on a Tuesday morning, and on Tuesday afternoon the full-time engineer called the employer to say that he was being admitted to the hospital that day for surgery. The full-time engineer would not be back to work for at least a month.

The business called the staffing service and asked if Nora could continue the temp assignment for the month the full-time engineer would be out sick. The service asked Nora about her availability to commit to a month-long assignment. Nora said she could work for two more weeks, but then she would need a few days off.

The business that needed Nora agreed to keep her for two more weeks and then let the service try to replace her for the days she needed off. The business liked Nora's work so much that it asked to have Nora back when she was once more available. Nora went into that particular temp job thinking she was filling in for an engineer who would be out a few days. She ended up extending her temp job there. That is the nature of temp work.

Special Projects

A special project could also be for an undetermined number of days. The duration of a special project will depend on the nature of the project you are working on. Some businesses do not know how long a special project will take when they ask a service to send them a temp. Many professional technical jobs, especially those in the field of information technology, may be start-up projects. A business may call a staffing service to send in skilled professional technical people to start up and complete a computer project. When you accept this type of job, it could last a day, week, months, or years.

Job Vacancy

If you are using temp work to find a full-time job, always ask the service if the temp job it is offering you has the potential to go full-time. Or, ask the service if the business is using a temp because it needs to hire someone full-time and the business has not hired someone yet.

If you know the type of permanent job you want, try to be even more selective about the types of temp jobs you take. For example, ask the service to find you temp jobs in the industry you want to work in, for the hours of the day you prefer, at the location that is best for you, and with pay that meets your salary requirements. Many people looking for permanent jobs have found their positions through temping. Look what happened to Judy.

Judy was looking for a permanent job as a bookkeeper. She knew she wanted her next full-time job to be one where she could utilize her knowledge of insurance claims and billing medical charges, along with her general bookkeeping skills. She asked the service where she applied for temporary work to offer her jobs as a bookkeeper in a hospital or with a medical practice.

The service had a request from a hospital for a temp to work in the business office as a bookkeeper. The hospital did not know if it was going to be able to fill the position full-time, because it was under a hiring freeze. But the hospital's business office had to complete its work and needed a temp to help.

The service offered the temp assignment to Judy. When she asked if the job might go full-time, the service shared with her the fact that the hospital was under a hiring freeze and did not know when it would be able to hire someone full-time. The service did tell her that the hospital had hired temps from the service for permanent jobs in the past and that she would be in a good position to get the job if she were already working in the hospital as a temp.

Judy decided to take a chance and go on that temp job at the hospital. She was glad she *did* go on the job, because she found out working in a hospital was nothing like she thought it would be, and she did not like it. She stayed at the hospital for two months and was then placed by the staffing service in a medical practice. Judy liked this temp job much better because the pace was different from the pace of the hospital, there were fewer people to work with, and she enjoyed using her skills a lot more.

This smaller office did not need another permanent employee (the full-time bookkeeper was on vacation), but the staff did know of another doctor's office that was looking to hire a permanent bookkeeper.

The medical practice recommended Judy to the other private practice that needed someone with her skills on a permanent basis. Judy accepted the job and would not have found it if she hadn't temped at the first medical office.

Why You Are on the Temp Job: The Staffing Service Markets the Skills of the Temp

THE SECOND WAY A SERVICE FINDS JOBS FOR YOU, A TEMP, IS BY CALLing businesses, telling them it has someone with your knowledge available, and asking the businesses if they need someone to work temp in that area.

Tim came to a service with skills as a drafter. The service where he applied had placed people with similar drafting skills at Business Z. The service called Business Z and said it had someone available to work temp with Tim's skills. Business Z asked the service to send Tim in the following Monday to do some temp work, and later offered him a full-time job as a drafter because he had done such a good job as a temp.

The service will try to match your skills to whatever temp jobs it has to fill. You may have several jobs to choose from or just one. You could be offered something that lasts one day, one week, one month, or several months. You may be offered day hours, evening hours, or weekend jobs. Remember, every temp job is different and may pay a different wage.

The key to getting the best temp job is to ask lots of questions and know what you want. Pay has been addressed extensively in Chapter 3 and will be briefly addressed here.

Pay

REMEMBER TO ASK, HOW MUCH DOES THE JOB PAY? REMEMBER, YOU will be taking home your hourly pay minus whatever has to be taken out for taxes and Social Security. Know your budget well. If you apply for temp work and you are offered $15 an hour for your first job, find out whether you will be offered that rate on every job or if your pay will be more or less than $15 an hour on future jobs.

When Paula applied for temp work as a bookkeeper with Satisfactory Staffing Service she knew she wanted to use her skills as a temp to find a permanent job. Satisfactory Staffing Service was very impressed with her test scores and her references and offered her a temp job as a bookkeeper with one of its best clients, a start-up company. Paula would be filling in for approximately six weeks for someone who would be on maternity leave.

Satisfactory Staffing Service offered Paula $14.50 an hour for the job. She was very eager to work and accepted the job. She temped well at the company and was a good representative for the service. At the end of six weeks, Satisfactory Staffing Service called Paula with another assignment, for two weeks, and she accepted the next temp job.

When Paula received her paycheck for the two-week job, she noticed her pay had decreased from $14.50 to $13.25. She immediately called the service to see why she was not receiving $14.50. The service told her they paid her $14.50 at the first company because it was a very important client and the service needed to send a top-notch temp.

The temp job where Paula was now was a small business that could not afford to pay the temp service as much money as the previous company. Therefore, the service could not pay her as much money. Paula was justifiably upset.

She should have asked how much money the service was offering her before accepting the two-week job. Never assume because you are paid one salary on one job that you will be paid the same on the next job. Always ask. Be your own best friend and make sure you are taking care of yourself financially. Do not sell yourself short.

Some services may negotiate with you up front as to what your rate of pay will be, and it will stay at the same rate no matter what the job is. You can ask for a raise when you gain more marketable skills. Just make sure you are happy with what you agree to.

Job Description

WHAT EXACTLY WILL YOU BE DOING? IS IT SOMETHING YOU WILL ENjoy doing and can do well, or is it something you need to tolerate doing for a few days in order to make some money? Can you do the job the service is asking you to do? If the service calls you with a job that is in your salary range, make sure you understand what you are being asked to do before you say yes.

Connie really wanted to work as a paralegal in the entertainment business in Los Angeles. She applied with Metropolitan Staffing Service, because they sent a lot of temps to companies in the entertainment business.

Metropolitan Staffing Service called Connie with a temp job working at a production company. The temp job required someone with acquisitions and mergers experience. Connie felt very confident about the position, and when the service asked her if she had transactional business experience, she wanted to work for the production company so much that she said yes.

When Connie arrived at the production company the next day, everyone on the legal staff was very uptight. They were relieved Connie was there, because they needed a qualified person to help complete a due diligence examination. This meant Connie was under a lot of pressure to perform well.

Connie did a good job organizing the documents, but could not figure out how to assess the significance of many of them. She was afraid to ask for help because she did not want anyone at the company to know she did not know how to get the work done.

Finally, someone from the production company asked Connie for a printout of what she had done so far. Connie confessed that she did not know how to do the work and that she wanted to work at the production company so much she had exaggerated her knowledge and experience to get her foot in the door.

Her supervisor at the production company was furious. He told Connie he would sign her time card for the hours she had been on the job so far that day, but that he wanted her to leave immediately. He said the production company had a very important deadline and that it was critical that the professional technical temp on this job be proficient.

In addition, the staffing service also believed Connie was a lost cause, justifiably fearing that her performance, or lack of performance, at the production company would hurt its reputation as a reliable staffing service for the entertainment business. The service was especially reluctant to offer Connie any jobs in the entertainment industry, because it appeared that she would say anything to get a temp job there and might not be a good representative of the service.

Make sure you understand what the service is asking you to do before you accept a temp job. If you get to the job and it is different from what the service described to you, call the person from the service who put you on the job as soon as possible.

Location

WHERE IS THE BUSINESS AT WHICH YOU WILL WORK LOCATED? CAN you get there easily? Will it be cost-effective for you to work there? Are you factoring in items like wardrobe, travel time, and parking when you agree to the salary? Will you have to relocate?

Working temp somewhere is just like working somewhere full-time. You need to make it cost-effective for you to work there. In other words, you do not want to spend more than you will make to get to work.

Check to make sure you can easily get to the place where the job is. The bank branch in San Jose where Pam was to report as a computer consultant at 8:00 A.M. was two miles from her home. Pam exited from the bus where the driver had suggested and quickly started walking to what she thought was her place of work. She arrived late with sore feet, having not worn shoes that were appropriate for walking the extra nine blocks when the bus driver let her out at the wrong place.

Pam should have made sure she understood exactly where the temp job was before she accepted the job. She should have asked the service for specific directions. If the service does not know the best way to travel between your home and the job site, make sure you take the time to plan your transportation. In such a case, it's a good idea to call the company itself. If Pam had called the company, she would have had better directions to the bank branch where she was supposed to report to work.

If you are driving, make sure you understand where you are going. Ask the service for written directions or a map showing you how to get to the place where the service is sending you to work. Be sure to give yourself plenty of time to get to work. Allow yourself extra time if you are unfamiliar with the area you are driving to. Remember, you will not make a good first impression if you are running late and do not get to your temp job on time.

Parking

IS PARKING PROVIDED BY THE BUSINESS OR THE SERVICE, OR WILL YOU be expected to pay for parking? Be sure to find this out, or you could be paying $5 to $20 out of your pocket in daily parking fees.

Some services never provide parking for their temps and tell the temps they will need to find parking facilities and pay for them on their own. Other services have agreements with the businesses they work with. Such agreements mean a business will provide so many parking places a month for temps, or will provide a temp with a parking pass that will not cost the temp any money.

George was assigned by a service to work as a physician's assistant at a clinic. The clinic where he was to work was in a high-rise building in the downtown area of the city where George lived. George was familiar with the building and drove there on his first day of the temp job. He had not asked the service where he was to park nor had the service mentioned parking to him, so George parked in the garage of the high-rise building.

At the end of George's first day at the clinic job, he asked the supervisor if she would stamp or verify his parking slip. The supervisor said it was not the policy of the clinic to provide or pay for temporary employees' parking. George turned his slip in to the parking lot attendant and was charged $22 for one day's parking. When he called the service about his parking situation, the service said its policy was that temporary employees had to pay for parking. George never asked about parking when he accepted the temp job at the clinic, and the staffing service assumed he knew he would have to find and pay for his own parking.

This was an expensive lesson for George. Always ask the service about parking before you accept a job. If you have to pay for parking, make sure you are being paid enough to make it worth your while. If you are not being paid enough, ask the service to pay you more to cover your parking.

Dress Code

Do you have the appropriate clothes to wear to the businesses where you will temp? It does not cost a lot of money to be clean and neat. Make sure you have a dark suit or dress if you will be working temp in a conservative business environment. Ask the service the type clothes full-time employees wear in the places where you are asked to work.

If you do not get any guidance from the service on how to dress, dress conservatively and professionally. That means a business suit for women and men. You can always change your attire the second day of the temp job if you are overdressed. It is better to make a good impression the first day by dressing more formally than necessary than to make a bad impression by dressing too casually.

Joseph accepted a temp job that started on a Friday in an insurance company in Hartford, Connecticut. Joseph was asked by the service to supervise the telemarketing for the insurance company; he would work on Friday as well as Monday through Friday of the following week. Joseph had read that many businesses observe a casual-dress day on Fridays, so he assumed he should dress casually on the first day of his job. You know what happened.

Joseph did not ask the service how to dress. The service's personnel assumed he would understand how he should dress when they explained what the job was and where he would be working. Joseph showed up in khakis and a knit golf shirt on the first day of his job. The executive vice president at the insurance company showed him where he would be working. Joseph observed that no one else was dressed casually. The executive vice president suggested to Joseph that they have lunch together that day.

At lunch the executive vice president said Joseph was doing a good job supervising the telemarketing, but that he would need to dress up on Monday if he wanted to continue the temp job. Joseph said he would wear a suit on Monday. The executive vice president said that particular insurance company observed casual day on the last Friday of each month and that he would tell the service about the casual-dress policy of the insurance company so that in the future no other temps would "dress down" when they were not supposed to.

Length of Assignment

HOW MANY DAYS DOES THE JOB LAST? IS IT FOR ONE DAY, ONE WEEK, one month, or a year, or is it an indefinite assignment? Every temp job is different. Do not assume that because you want to work Monday through Friday that every temp job you accept will meet your needs.

Be sure to ask the person from the service who offers you a temp job how long the job will last. Many times the service will not know the length of the temp job it offers you because the business that has requested a temp does not know how long it will need someone to work. Often, the length of the job depends on how long it takes a temp to finish the work given to him or her to do.

If you are filling in for someone who is out sick, you will be there until the person you are filling in for is well. That could be one day or two months.

If you are working a temp job that is open because there is a job vacancy, you could be asked to temp until someone is hired full-time for the job. You may like the job and do such a good job that *you* will be the person hired for the job full-time.

Write down on your calendar whatever the service tells you is the length of the job. If you are a successful professional, the staffing services will have numerous client jobs for you, and your calendar will fill rapidly. Make sure you can be there the days you have committed to work. If the service asks you to work two weeks and you are available only one week, tell the service immediately. The service may ask you to go on the job for one week and then replace you with another temp in the second week, or the service may find a job that is exactly the length you say you are available to work.

The reason you have chosen to work temp is to earn money while you enjoy the flexibility of temporary jobs. If you are available only Monday and Wednesday of one week, do not accept a job that would require you to work Tuesday and Thursday also.

Meg had been working temp through National Staffing Service for four months. She had developed a good working relationship with National Staffing Service and had made the service look good at various places where she temped for them. Meg had set aside a Wednesday to go to the dentist, get a checkup with her doctor, and have her car serviced. Meg told the staffing service she could work on Monday, Tuesday, and Thursday for them because she needed Wednesday off, and she also planned to take Friday off so she could leave town for a long weekend.

The service found Meg a job that was for Monday and Tuesday only that week. The service called her Thursday morning and sent her out to a job that day as well. By communicating what her schedule was, Meg was able to work with the service to find her jobs on the days she was available to work.

Brian, on the other hand, was not honest with his service about when he was really available for temp work. Brian had been doing a good job with Contemporary Staffing Service. The service asked him to work Monday through Friday for a business, and Brian agreed to do so without telling the service he needed Friday off to go out of town. The service called Brian on Thursday afternoon to offer him another temp job starting the following Monday. Brian accepted the job.

The following morning, Friday, Brian called the service and told them he was sick and would not be able to complete the job. The service sounded sympathetic and sent another temp in to finish out the week of the job Brian was on. Brian left town.

People from the service tried to call Brian on Friday afternoon and over the weekend. When they did not hear from Brian, they left word on his answering machine that they assumed he was too sick to work on Monday, since he had not returned any of the service's phone calls, and the service was replacing him with another temp. If Brian had been honest and told the service he could only work through Thursday, it would have worked with his schedule. By not being direct with the service, he lost out on a good temp job that had the chance of going permanent and that started the following Monday.

Communication Is Important!

SOME ONE-DAY JOBS END UP LASTING MUCH LONGER. BE SURE TO communicate with your service if a business asks you to stay longer than the service has scheduled you to work there. That way the service knows exactly what days you are working and can continue to offer you jobs on the days you are available to work. If you do not communicate with the service, you will miss being offered jobs where you can make money and potentially find full-time work.

Mark was sent by a service to work for two days at a college that needed an administrator to help with an unexpectedly large number of admission applications. The college had requested a temp for two days to help finish this special project. During the afternoon of the second day Mark was on the temp job, the college staff realized the project would take longer than they had expected and decided they would need to keep a temp for more than two days.

The college called the service to see if it could extend Mark's assignment. When the service had sent Mark to work for the college, he had been uncertain about his future availability for temp work. He told the service he did not think he could work any longer than two days and did not know when he would be available for any temp work in the near future.

The service did not try to call Mark to see if he wanted to continue past two days for the college where he was working. Mark did not call the service at the end of the second day to see if the service had another job for him.

The service offered the administrative job to another temp. Mark was disappointed because he liked the work. The college staff were disappointed because they wanted to keep Mark. The service should have called Mark first and at least told him that the college really liked his performance and wanted him to continue his temp job.

The lesson is always to take the initiative about your availability by calling the service and making sure your temp assignment is ending on the day the service tells you it is going to end. The more you communicate with the staffing service, the more frequently you will work.

Hours

WHEN ARE YOU TO REPORT TO WORK? MAKE SURE YOU KNOW THE hours you are expected to be on the job so that you can be on time.

If you need to work day hours, ask the service to offer you those hours. If you already have another job, ask the service to help you with jobs that will allow you to keep your first job.

Supervisor on the Job

WHOM DO YOU REPORT TO AT THE BUSINESS WHERE YOU WILL TEMP? Get a name and phone number in case you get lost or need directions. This information will also be helpful for your family in case of emergency and if your family needs to reach you.

Supervisor from the Staffing Service

MAKE SURE YOU KNOW WHO YOUR CONTACT IS AT THE STAFFING service. That person should be your point of reference when you need help. If you have any questions about your job assignment, your pay, or any benefits, make sure you know whom to call. Keep that person's phone number with you. Many staffing services that place professional technical employees have answering services. Do not hesitate to call the staffing service, at any hour of the day, should you need help. Remember, the staffing service will make money only when you go to work. The staffing service should want to keep you happy so that you will continue to work and make money for it.

CHAPTER FOURTEEN

Your First Day on the Job as a Professional Technical Temp

(How to Make What Could Be a Painful Experience a Fun One)

YOU HAVE ACCEPTED YOUR FIRST TEMP JOB. YOU ARE EXCITED AND scared. You should be. Starting a temp job is like starting any new job. The only difference between starting a temp job and starting a full-time job is the full-time job lasts longer. If you change temp jobs every week, you will have to go through the same process every week that someone who changes full-time jobs may go through every few years.

Review Your Directions

GIVE YOURSELF PLENTY OF EXTRA TIME TO GET TO WORK ON YOUR first day. Allow yourself time to be caught in a traffic jam, change your panty hose because you have a run in them, or change a flat tire. If you have not been there previously, drive to the company the day before you are to start work to find out exactly where the job is. That way you will know where you are going and will not get lost the first day you are to be there.

Know the person's name you are to report to. This person may be your supervisor for your temp job or it could be the assistant to the person who will actually oversee your work. Write that person's name and phone number down so that you will have something to refer to in case you forget. You should also write down the name of the company and the company's address for the same reasons.

Once You Get There

IF YOU ARRIVE EARLY, WAIT IN THE LOBBY UNTIL SOMEONE FROM THE business gets there. If someone (like a receptionist) comes out to greet you, say what staffing service you are from and whom you are to report to. Some companies work with several services, so never assume the staffing service you represent is the only service that sends temps to that business.

A business may have a security guard who asks everyone who works there to sign a register. The guard will need to know what service you are with, and you should also tell the guard what department and supervisor you are there to work for.

You may be asked to wait in the lobby until someone can escort you to your place of work. You may also be given a parking pass or a badge like other employees of the company wear.

Orientation Films and Brochures

AN ORIENTATION PROCESS IS A PROCEDURE THAT INFORMS YOU ABOUT the company where you are working. Some companies may have an orientation film to view or a brochure to read before you start work. It will tell you what the product of the company is, who its customers are, what the policies are, and how you will fit in. That is why the process is called an orientation—because it orients or introduces you to the company.

The company may ask you to sign a document that verifies you have read its brochure or watched its film. If you are given a badge or a pass, you will be responsible for turning it back in at the end of your assignment.

Confidentiality

DUE TO THE IMPORTANT NATURE OF MANY PROFESSIONAL, EXECU-tive, or technical temp jobs, you may have access to valuable data that the company considers proprietary. Do not be surprised if the company asks you to sign a legally binding nondisclosure agreement.

Getting Direction versus Being Left on Your Own (Sink or Swim)

YOU MAY BE ASSIGNED TO A SMALL BUSINESS THAT DOES NOT HAVE any formal policy for temps working on its premises. In fact, you may start work the second you walk in the door. You may have to fig-ure out how to do the job by yourself. Look what happened to two different people on their first day at a temp job.

Sam reported to XYZ Computing Company, having been sent by a staffing service to work as a consulting manager. When he ar-rived at 7:55 A.M. on his first day (he was to start work at 8:00 A.M.), no one was at the front desk. He could see where the receptionist was to sit and work, and he heard phones ringing. Sam sat waiting for in-structions.

At 8:10 A.M., Damon, one of the employees of XYZ, arrived. He nodded to Sam and hurried down the hall to another office. About five minutes later Damon came back, carrying his coffee mug, and asked Sam if he had been helped. Sam said no, he was there to work as a temp and was waiting to report to Mr. Nelson. Damon verified Sam's status and had him sign a confidentiality agreement.

Damon said Mr. Nelson would not be in that day, pointed Sam in the direction of the office area specializing in client-server tools and relational database management systems (RDBMSs) modeling, and wished Sam luck.

Sam spent the rest of the day greeting other consulting managers in the division but never received any guidance as to his position's goals or needs.

Sam had to figure out how to do things himself on his first day at

XYZ because the person who was to supervise him never showed up. Sometimes, as a temp, you just have to make things up as you go along because no one may be there to show you how to do them. You may not get any feedback or direction at the place you are sent to work.

If you do not know what to do, call your service and ask the person who put you on the job for suggestions. That is one of the things a staffing service gets paid to do—figure things out when no one is there from the business to help you. Make it be the service's headache, not yours.

Sarah had a different experience from Sam on her first day. Sarah reported to a large bank that had very specific instructions for temps. The service had given Sarah a manual to read about the bank before she started work there. The manual told her where to park, what the dress code was, the standards for bank employees, who the bank's customers were, and what the mission statement was for the bank.

Sarah followed the manual's instructions about how to get to the bank and parked her car where she was supposed to park. She reported to a guard station, signed in, and waited for her designated supervisor. The supervisor came to the guard station and escorted her to the place where she was to work.

Sarah had been told by the service she would be working as an information system auditor. The supervisor showed Sarah where she would be working and then sat beside her for a few hours to make sure she had all of her questions answered and was comfortable. Several people in the department where Sarah was working stopped by and introduced themselves. Sarah had very few problems adjusting to her temp work as a result.

Questions to Ask

NO MATTER HOW YOU ARE GREETED BY THE BUSINESS ON THE FIRST day, try to make the best of it. Ask questions and get instructions from whoever your supervisor is. If your supervisor is very busy, try to time your questions for when he or she appears to be less busy.

Organizational Chart

Many companies have an organizational chart that they give to temps. This will help you learn names and who is in what position, as well as learn how the company is structured.

Ask for Feedback

Even if you are working in a very busy, fast-paced environment, it is important to find out as soon as possible whether you are doing your job correctly. If your work needs to be corrected or you need to change the way you are doing things, it is better to find that out sooner than later. Most businesses will appreciate your initiative and your willingness to try to do the right thing to please them.

Breaks

Some businesses have a set time for you to take a break. This could be a 15-minute break in the morning or a 15-minute break in the afternoon. Or, you may be expected by the business where you are temping to say when you need a break. Make sure you talk to your service and find out how you are to document such a break on your time card.

Lunch or Dinner

There may be a set time that you are expected to take lunch or dinner in order for the office to be adequately staffed. Find out when you are to take lunch so that you will be informed (and your stomach will know when it will be fed). Are you to take 30 minutes, 45 minutes, or an hour for this meal? Be sure to document on your time card the time you are not working.

Telephone Extensions Directory

If you are going to be on the assignment more than a day, it will help if you have a list of people's extensions so that you know how to call them.

Use of the Phone

Some companies are very strict about the use of their phones for personal calls. If you need to make a phone call, play it safe and ask permission. Your service may want you to call when you have arrived at your place of work. You may need to give a member of your family a number where you can be reached. Do not abuse the use of the phone. Nothing aggravates an employer like having an employee talking on the phone with personal business during work hours instead on concentrating on work.

Get Help

IF YOU START A JOB AND DON'T UNDERSTAND IT, STOP AND ASK FOR directions. If you cannot get any feedback, make a call to the staffing service and ask the person who placed you on the job to help you. Many times the service can get feedback for you very quickly, because it has worked with the business before and may be familiar with the tasks you are doing.

Janet was assigned to a temp job by Quality Staffing Service. The service told Janet she would be working for Better Financial Services as a reference data administrator.

Quality Staffing Service and Better Financial Services had a contract that said any temp sent to Better Financial Services had to read an employee handbook and sign a document saying the temp had read the book. It was the responsibility of Quality Staffing Service to make sure the temps read the book and signed the document. That meant Quality Staffing Service was responsible for the orientation of any temps the service sent to Better Financial Services. The handbook explained the mission and philosophy of Better Financial.

Janet reported to the receptionist at Better Financial on her first day. The receptionist told her the vice president, Paul, would come and escort her to the place where she would be working.

Paul walked Janet to the work area and Janet noticed it was very busy, that each employee had his or her own computer station. Paul took Janet to the station where she would be working for the next week and showed her how to turn on the computer, how to log in, and how to use the phone set. He also introduced her to some of the people working around her. He showed Janet where his office was and told her to come and get him or dial his extension if she needed help.

After three days, Janet showed Paul a preliminary outline of the changes she proposed for the company's common reference data. Janet asked Paul to review her work so that she would know if she was on the right track.

Paul noticed one mistake and showed Janet how to correct it. He thanked her for taking the initiative to show him her work. He reviewed her work at the end of the day and made very few changes. By taking the time to ask someone to review her work and by asking questions, Janet was able to remove some of the stress and anxiety she was feeling.

It is a fact that some companies do not make it easy for temps to do their jobs. This lack of support is especially hard for people new to temping who want to do a good job and make a good impression. Some people view temps as second-class coworkers and do not think it is worth their time to communicate with temps and give them feedback on their jobs. That is a loss for people with this type of attitude, because temporary workers are here to stay. The more people communicate with temps and give them feedback about their job performance, the better the output for everyone at the company.

Do's and Don'ts

IT'S NOT ENOUGH JUST TO BE TECHNICALLY PROFICIENT.

Do—be punctual and on time to work. If you are late on the first day, that may be the only thing your supervisor remembers about you, no matter how well you perform your temp job.

Do—observe the dress code. Try to fit in. You do not want to be conspicuous and stand out because you wore the wrong clothes. Your good work will be overlooked if you are not dressed appropriately.

Do—be friendly, smile, and introduce yourself. If you have the right attitude, the people where you temp are more likely to help you succeed.

Do—pay attention to the instructions your supervisor where you report to work gives you. Make sure you understand what you are asked to do. Your assignment will go much better if you do not have to repeat a task because you did not know how to do it right the first time.

Do—ask questions; be persistent.

Don't—be rude or have bad manners. People will remember how you misbehaved long after you are gone.

Don't—smoke indiscriminately. Many buildings have policies against smoking on the premises. If you want to smoke, make sure you know where the designated smoking area is. If there is not such an area, do not smoke at all.

Don't—read newspapers or magazines at your workstation unless you are on a break. If someone sees you reading a book (other than this one) that does not relate to work, the company may question its need for your services and say it cannot afford to pay someone to read instead of work. The business could then call the service and send you home because you do not appear to be busy.

Don't—suffer in silence. If you really do not like something about your job, call the service as soon as possible. It needs feedback from you.

CHAPTER FIFTEEN

What to Do If You Hate Your Temp Job

(And How to Get Out of a Temp Job You Hate and into One You Will Like)

Do Not Tolerate Discrimination or Harassment

IF YOU ARE EVER PLACED ON A JOB WHERE YOU FEEL THAT YOU ARE BEing discriminated against, harassed, or mistreated, get up and leave the office immediately, and call or go see your service as soon as possible. Never stay in a place where you are not safe. If the service does not respond in a satisfactory way, report it to the Equal Employment Opportunity Commission (EEOC) or consult an attorney.

Organizations for Specific Problems

WHILE STAFFING SERVICES SHOULD OFFER FAIR TREATMENT WITHOUT regard to race, color, national origin, religion, sex, age, or disability, you should be aware of your legal rights. The organizations listed below provide information on career planning, training, job opportunities, or public policy support for specific groups and concerns. If you believe a staffing service has discriminated against you or failed to enforce your legal rights, these organizations can be a valuable resource, and you may want to consider contacting the Equal Employment Opportunity Commission as well as any of the following:

People with Disabilities

The President's Committee on Employment of People with Disabilities can be reached at 1331 F Street NW, 3rd Floor, Washington, DC 20004; telephone (202) 376-6200.

The Blind

Information on the free national reference and referral service provided by the Federation of the Blind can be obtained by contacting Job Opportunities for the Blind (JOB), National Federation of the Blind, 1800 Johnson Street, Baltimore, MD 21230; telephone (410) 659-9314 or toll-free 1-800-638-7518.

Minorities

The National Association for the Advancement of Colored People (NAACP) is located at 4805 Mount Hope Drive, Baltimore, MD 21215; telephone (410) 358-8900.

The National Urban League is a nonprofit community-based social service and civil rights organization that assists African-Americans in the achievement of social and economic equality. There are 113 local affiliates throughout the United States that provide services related to employment and job training, education, and career development. Contact the affiliate nearest you for information.

Older Workers

American Association of Retired Persons, Workforce Program Department, 601 E Street NW, Floor A5, Washington, DC 20049; telephone (202) 434-2040.

Asociación Nacional por Personas Mayores (National Association for Hispanic Elderly), 2727 West 6th Street, Suite 270, Los Angeles, CA 90057; telephone (213) 487-1922. (This organization specifically serves low-income, minority persons who are 55 years of age and older.)

National Association of Older Workers Employment Services, c/o

National Council on the Aging, 409 3rd Street SW, Suite 200, Washington, DC 20024; telephone (202) 479-1200.

National Caucus/Center on Black Aged, Inc., 1424 K Street NW, Suite 500, Washington, DC 20005; telephone (202) 637-8400.

Veterans

Contact the nearest regional office of the U.S. Department of Veterans Affairs or contact Veterans' Employment and Training Service (VETS), 200 Constitution Avenue NW, Room S-1315, Washington, DC 20210; telephone (202) 219-9116.

Women

Catalyst, 250 Park Avenue South, 5th Floor, New York, NY 10003; telephone (212) 777-8900.

U.S. Department of Labor, Women's Bureau, 200 Constitution Avenue NW, Washington, DC 20210; telephone (202) 219-6652.

Wider Opportunities for Women, 815 15th Street NW, Suite 916, Washington, DC 20005; telephone (202) 638-3143.

Federal laws, executive orders, and selected federal grant programs bar discrimination in employment based on race, color, national origin, religion, sex, age, and handicap. Information on how to file a charge of discrimination is available from the U.S. Equal Employment Opportunity Commission offices around the country. Their addresses and telephone numbers are listed in telephone directories under U.S. Government, EEOC, or are available from: Equal Employment Opportunity Commission, 1801 L Street NW, Washington, DC 20507; telephone (202) 663-4900 or (202) 275-7377.

Information on federal laws concerning fair labor standards such as the minimum wage and equal employment opportunity can be obtained from Office of Public Affairs, Employment Standards Administration, U.S. Department of Labor, Room C-4325, 200 Constitution Avenue NW, Washington, DC 20210; telephone (202) 219-8743.

Communicate with Your Staffing Service

WHAT IF YOU ARE IN A JOB WHERE EVERYTHING IS LEGAL, BUT YOU just do not like the job? How can you get out of that job and move to one you will like?

You should communicate with the person from the staffing service who placed you on the job. The staffing service needs to know exactly what you do not like about the job so that another job can be found for you that you will like.

You need to explain why you do not like the job. Is it because of the type of work you are expected to do? For example, if you are placed on a job as a paralegal and the business asks you to answer the telephone as a receptionist, you need to tell the staffing service you do not want to do that type of work; you were sent to the job as a paralegal and that is what you expect to be. Many times, the staffing service is not given all the facts by a business that requests a temp.

The staffing service and the business need to communicate anytime there is a change in a job description that involves you, the temp. It could also mean a change in pay for you.

Helen was sent by the Amazing Staffing Service to work as a marketing consultant for a month at the corporate headquarters of a national bookstore chain. The service told her she would be analyzing the chain's customer base for a special project. When Helen started her job she realized she was not going to like the work. The office was too busy, the atmosphere was chaotic, and she was expected to do the work of five people. The reason the bookstore called the Amazing Staffing Service was because Helen's predecessor had walked off the job without giving any notice several days before and the bookstore had not tried to hire anyone else.

Helen's nerves were shot by midmorning of the first day at the bookstore office. She called the person from the staffing service who had placed her on the job and said she was not going to be able to complete the assignment. She told the service that the job was too stressful for her, all the executives were yelling at her, the phones never stopped ringing, and she could not concentrate on her project.

She also said the bookstore office expected her to go and get everyone's lunch during her lunch break.

The service asked Helen if she would stay until the end of business hours and finish the day at the bookstore office. The staffing service said if Helen would stay until 5:00 P.M. it would replace her at the bookstore office and find her another job that would better suit her. Helen agreed to stay until the end of the day, and was placed by the staffing service at a job the next day working in a less stressful and better structured environment. The staffing service talked to its contact at the bookstore office, who said the bookstore chain really needed a temp who was looking for full-time work and would be interested in staying with the company. The service replaced Helen with another temp who only wanted to work temp and was not looking for full-time employment but who did like books and a fast-paced work style and was a marketing whiz.

The staffing service was able to get the bookstore headquarters to use this temp while the service sent over other people for the bookstore office to interview who were looking for full-time jobs. That way, the work was getting done while the bookstore office could take the time to select the right person to stay with it for the full-time work. The situation worked out to be a win-win for everyone because Helen communicated.

The service should have taken the time to investigate why the bookstore office needed a temp and should have known that Helen would not be a good match for the bookstore even on a temporary basis. If the staffing service had not agreed to find Helen a replacement, she could have opted to leave the bookstore job on the first day and gone to sign up with another staffing service that would listen to what her needs were.

If Helen had left the job at the bookstore headquarters without communicating with the Amazing Staffing Service, then the service could have terminated her employment with them for walking off the job. Anytime you leave a job without communicating with the staffing service that placed you there you run the risk of being fired by the service. Staffing services fire temps just like full-time employers do.

You Can Fire Your Staffing Service

THE MORE YOU TEMP, THE MORE COMFORTABLE YOU WILL BE WITH giving your staffing service feedback. If the service does not take the time to listen to you and work with you, it is telling you that you are not important to it and it does not value your work. Staffing services do not succeed without good temps. So, if one staffing service is not good for you, then you, the temp, should fire it and change to a service that does appreciate you. Remember, the temporary employment business is very competitive, and services are competing for good temps just like they compete for the best companies to send the temps to. People who temp talk to other temps and they talk to businesses that hire temps. Services should treat their temps right; the staffing service that does not deserves to have a bad reputation in the temporary industry.

Change staffing services if your current service doesn't help you, and tell everyone why you fired the service. If you like the business where the staffing service placed you and the service is mistreating you, tell the business you want to keep working there but you will have to be hired through another staffing service, and tell the business what service you are switching to. (Most companies work with more than one staffing service, so the business may even recommend another staffing service that would help you more than the current staffing service has done.) If any staffing service does not treat you well, the service does not deserve to work with you. Find a staffing service that does deserve to make money from your services.

Talk to Other Professional Technical Temps

IF YOU SEE ANOTHER TEMP DOING A JOB YOU WANT TO DO, ASK THE temp how he or she got the job. If the temp is working through the same staffing service you are, call the service and see if you are qualified for the job. Tell the staffing service you want the next opportunity to do that job.

If the temp on the job is working through another staffing service, call that service and go apply with them. Be specific with the service about why you are there and say which job you want.

The staffing service you are currently working through may ask you to continue with the job you are on that you do not like until it can replace you and find you the job you want. It is up to you whether you will stay on a job you do not like while waiting for one to open that you will like.

CHAPTER SIXTEEN

Ways to Turn That Temp Job into a Full-Time Job

(Or, How to Fool the Staffing Service)

WORKING AS A TEMP IN ORDER TO FIND A PERMANENT FULL-time professional career used to be frowned upon by the staffing services, but then they got smart and started negotiating a signed agreement with the employer so as to receive a fee when a temp professional was hired as a regular employee. Consequently, temps no longer have to subvert their present employer or engage in subterfuge when seeking to transfer from temp work to permanent work. As personnel expert Carol Kleiman of the *Chicago Tribune* wrote March 16, 1997, "Today, the transition from 'temp to hire' is out in the open with full approval from all involved. What's more, some employers are hiring staff on a temporary basis as a means of evaluating them for full-time jobs."

In a recent study of over 150 human resource and personnel managers at the nation's top 1000 companies, OfficeTeam, a national staffing service, reported that companies used the temp-to-hire procedure about 23% of the time. The study found that employers actually offered permanent jobs to temps almost 40% of the time but many of the temps declined, so as to reduce the temp-to-hire average to 23%. Another recent study by Manpower, Inc., a staffing service that employs 750,000 persons, found that over 40% of Manpower's temps have become employed permanently by the client companies.

Many of you are working temp to find a permanent job. There

are ways to use temp work to your advantage and network your way to the job you want.

Work a Variety of Temp Jobs

IF YOU DO NOT KNOW WHAT YOU WANT TO DO WHEN YOU GROW UP (and who does?) you should work a variety of temp jobs and see what you like the most. One week you might work in a publishing house, the next week in a bank, and the following week in a law firm or medical practice.

There is no teacher like experience to show you what the real world is like. Many people have preconceived ideas about what a certain job will be like only to be disappointed when they actually get the job. If you temp in a position you might be interested in, you do not have the commitment you would have if you had accepted the job as a permanent position. You can simply ask the staffing service to change your assignment and keep changing the assignment until the service matches you with a job you like.

Choose the Staffing Service That Can Maximize Your Opportunities!

YOU SHOULD BE WORKING WITH A STAFFING SERVICE THAT HAS A good reputation and has successfully placed temps in the kind of job you want. For example, if you want an accounting job, make sure you are working with a staffing service that has lots of job orders for temps in accounting and has successfully placed people in temp-to-permanent jobs.

Debbie had completed three years at Vanderbilt University and was working toward a degree in accounting. She decided to spend the summer before her senior year of college working as a temp on accounting jobs. She signed up with a staffing service and was placed on two accounting jobs that summer. Each job lasted approximately six weeks, and Debbie was able to use many of the skills she had been taught in school and also used her accounting computer skills.

The first job was in a big corporate accounting firm. The work was very structured and left little room for individual contribution. Debbie felt very stifled there. The second job was a better match for Debbie. She worked for a small company that sold equipment to factories. The company was starting to grow but was still small enough for the employees to pay attention to each other.

Debbie decided when she graduated from college to ask the staffing service to place her in another company similar to her second job. Debbie also asked the equipment company to keep her resume on file for any permanent opening it might have. Debbie called the equipment company all through her last year of college and the company offered her a full-time job after her college graduation.

Know Which Businesses the Staffing Service Works For

ANOTHER WAY TO TURN A TEMP JOB INTO A FULL-TIME JOB IS TO GET the company where you want to work to request you as a temp. In order to do that you need to find out what staffing service the company uses for temps.

If you go to a company where you want a full-time job you may be directed to the company's personnel office. The personnel office may tell you the company is not taking applications at that time. What you can do if you really want to work there is ask if the company uses temporary employees. If the answer is yes, find out if the company has its own in-house temporary pool. If the company has an in-house pool of temps, it interviews, recruits, and manages people who work temp there.

But if the company tells you it uses a staffing service, find out which service is used. Then go sign up with that staffing service. Be very specific when you sign up with the staffing service and tell the service you chose it in order to be placed as a temp with a specific business. Explain to the staffing service that you want to be sent on temp jobs at that business and that you prefer temp jobs that have the possibility to go permanent.

However, you should not limit yourself to only temp jobs at that business that are temp-to-perm. Try to be open to taking any temp job in the company you want to work for permanently so that you can get exposure to the company. The more you work as a temp in the company, the more people who will see you. The more people who see you, the better your exposure will be. If you do a good job, you will increase your chances of getting a permanent job in that company. Many times getting the permanent job you want is the result of being in the right place at the right time.

Don't forget to check in with the personnel office on a regular basis while you are temping in the company where you want to work full-time. Do not make a pest of yourself; calling or stopping by the personnel office twice a month is a good rule of thumb. This will show the personnel office you are serious and eager about working at the company full-time. Make your visits or phone calls short and friendly; do not waste the personnel office's time.

Remember to check in with your staffing service on a regular basis about your progress with the company where you want a full-time job. If the staffing service has you working somewhere else, make sure you are only obligated for a short-term job so that you can be ready to go on the next available temp job the staffing service has with your target company. Your other temp jobs should be no longer than a week in length.

If you are already temping at the company where you want a full-time job, ask the staffing service for a progress report. Get the staffing service to talk to its contacts in the company and see what kind of feedback the staffing service gets from the company. If the company tells the staffing service you are a good temp but are not going to be a match for the company on a permanent basis, get the staffing service to find out why. If the staffing service can give you feedback that will help you meet your goal of full-time employment, you should take advantage of it.

Peter was a newly licensed CPA who wanted a permanent job with Merged & Acquired Bank. When he asked the personnel office if he could submit his resume and fill out an application he was told that

Merged & Acquired Bank was not taking new applications. The personnel office told him it would keep his resume on file for six months and call him if there was a job opening that matched his qualifications during that period. The receptionist also told him the bank had a phone line that was dedicated for job openings; he could call that phone line to find out what the bank might be actively recruiting for.

Peter was serious about wanting to work for Merged & Acquired Bank; he had learned that Merged & Acquired Bank had a reputation for promoting people who worked hard. He asked the receptionist whether the bank used temps, and the receptionist replied that she was a temp from Quality Staffing Service. He then inquired whether Quality Staffing Service provided all of the temps for the bank. The receptionist was not sure, but suggested Peter try to check the sign-in sheet at the guard station where all temps had to sign in each day and also list which staffing service they worked for. Not all check-in stations are easy to check for temp listings. But Peter was persistent, and he was able to see that 10 temps had signed in to work on that particular day and that 6 of the 10 were from Quality Staffing Service, 2 were from Superior Staffing, and 2 were from Backup Staffing Company.

Peter then registered with all three staffing services. He was very direct with each of them, explaining that he was temping to get his foot in the door of Merged & Acquired Bank. He requested temp jobs that had the potential to go full-time but said he would not rule out any professional, executive, or technical temp assignment at that particular bank.

Quality Staffing Service told Peter the only job it had open that day with the bank was as an auditor in a job that would last only 10 days. The service expected to get more jobs open with the bank but was not sure when. Superior Staffing Service told Peter it could offer him a temp job with the bank assisting the collections manager starting the next day and lasting about a month. Backup Staffing Service said Merged & Acquired Bank called them only when Quality Staffing Service or Superior Staffing Service could not fill temp jobs, but Backup Staffing wanted to offer Peter a temp job at another bank that was long-term and could go full-time.

Peter had a decision to make. He had already decided to focus on getting a permanent job at Merged & Acquired Bank. Which temp job would help him achieve his goal? He decided to take the Quality Staffing Service offer and see what other types of jobs it had to fill for the bank in the future. Peter's decision was based on the fact that Quality Staffing Service sent more temps to the bank than any other staffing service; he therefore believed he had the best chance of getting a full-time job with the bank with this staffing service.

About a week after working the 10-day auditor job, Peter received a call from Quality Staffing Service saying there was an investment analyst position available in the trust department of the bank. The temp position with the bank was available because the trust department had several extra projects to do and the bank was reluctant to hire more full-time employees to do the work. The bank decided to get the projects started by hiring temps and then see if the amount of work would justify hiring these temps full-time.

Peter accepted this temp job with Quality Staffing Service. His research had told him the trust department was a very prestigious place to work in the bank. Peter knew he could meet many movers and shakers in the bank, because the trust department was responsible for a lot of money. He decided to dress like the other full-time bank employees and to copy as many of the good work habits of his coworkers as he could.

Peter worked as a temp for three months at Merged & Acquired Bank. During those three months he talked to his supervisor, Pamela, at Quality Staffing Service at least once every two weeks. He asked her to give him any feedback about what his chances were of being hired full-time by the bank. He wrote a letter each month to the bank personnel office to remind them of his interest in joining the bank. He also checked in with the personnel department of the bank twice a month in person. He was friendly and professional.

In addition, Peter wrote a thank-you note to his supervisor at Quality Staffing Service. He knew Pamela supervised a lot of temps at the bank and he did not want her to forget about him. Pamela appreciated Peter's enthusiasm and professional attitude, and she did not receive any complaints about him from the bank. He was good at his work, punctual, dressed appropriately, had good work habits, and took direction well. He also asked questions when he needed direction.

When after three months the bank decided to end the projects in the trust department that meant Peter's temp job in that department of the bank was concluded. Because he had continued to remind Pamela how much he want to work at that bank, she went out of her way to find another job for him there.

The bank personnel office told Pamela the bank had a full-time job opening in the internal audit department. The bank was impressed with the skills Peter had shown in the trust department. Pamela talked the bank into trying Peter out, and so the bank agreed to try him in internal audit for a period of eight weeks. At the end of that time, if the bank and Peter were working well together, Peter would become a full-time employee of the bank. And that is what happened.

Make Your Staffing Service Your Cheerleader!

THE POINT OF PETER'S STORY IS THAT AS A PROFESSIONAL TECHNICAL temp, you may have to sell yourself to the staffing service that can help you land the full-time job you want. That means you need to make a good friend of the representative from the staffing service who can help you the most.

Find out which supervisor handles the company where you want to work. Ask to meet that supervisor in person. If you cannot meet that person, at least get an appointment on the phone with him or her. That supervisor is the one who will determine whether you get a chance for a full-time job in the company where you want to work. Send a thank-you note for speaking with you. Find out what day the supervisor's birthday is and sent a card or call. Ask about hobbies and family. Let the supervisor know you care about him or her as a person.

Remember, many staffing services demand a lot from their employees, which means the employees are constantly trying to balance recruiting temps, paying temps, and selling their services to businesses. Anything you can do to distinguish yourself in a positive way from other temps will be a plus for you. Your supervisor will work harder to find you the right job, and may also tell other people in the staffing service to help you. It can make all the difference in the world for you whether you get a mediocre temp job or one that will let your talents shine.

Write the president or owner of the staffing service and compliment the person who has been helpful to you. People appreciate compliments in writing. Many times these compliments are filed in the personnel file of the person you are writing about and are used as reasons to give people a raise. People at staffing services who are popular with the temporaries they manage should be paid a financial reward and you, the temp, can help make that happen.

As a result, you should be treated well and be given good temp jobs.

Send the person who sends you on temp jobs a thank-you note. Your thoughtfulness will be appreciated and you will be remembered when the next really good temp-to-perm job comes along.

Be Reliable

THE MORE DEPENDABLE YOU ARE, THE BETTER TEMP JOBS YOU WILL get. When you agree to work for a staffing service, you are an employee of the staffing service. When you do your job well, you make the staffing service look good in the eyes of the businesses that hire the staffing service. The better you make the staffing service look, the more likely the staffing service is to offer you the best temp jobs.

Many staffing services will emphasize when you sign on as a temp that you are to show up for work when you say you will. If you do not show up for work or are late several times, the staffing service will not send you out on the best jobs, and may even choose to fire you.

The good jobs will go to temps who are punctual and reliable. So remember, if you want the best jobs, be reliable. Give the staffing service plenty of notice if you are going to be late or if you are sick. (But be warned that some staffing services will be very hesitant to use temps who call in sick frequently.) Do not overcommit yourself or say you will work if you are sick. You are better off telling the staffing service you will call when you are well rather than saying you will be at work when you are unable to do so.

Emergencies do happen, and many staffing services will work with you in case of emergency. Most staffing services have answering services that will give messages to the person who is your supervisor. You can call these answering services during the middle of the night or on weekends and leave word for your contact if you have an emergency and will be unable to be at work. The next business day, you should call to make sure your contact got the message; then call once you know when the emergency will be over and find out when you can report back to work.

The more responsible you are, the more respect you will get from the service and from businesses where you want a permanent job.

Don't forget that many prospective employers call services and check your references. If you have not been truthful, reliable, or dependable, you cannot expect a good reference from the staffing service. Peter, the CPA, could also have asked his supervisors at Merged & Acquired Bank to tell Pamela, his service supervisor, what a good job he was doing so that she would want to send him back to the bank as a temp.

On completing a temp assignment at a company, be sure to send your supervisor there a thank-you note and put in writing how much you enjoyed working for him or her. If the supervisor is with a company where you want a permanent job, enclose a resume and ask for his or her help. The supervisor may know about a potential job that you would be perfect for. Remember, it is often whom you know, not what you know, that could get you the job you want. Take advantage of every suitable opportunity you have to get your name in front of the right people. Just make sure you do it in the right place and at the appropriate time.

Ask for Letters of Recommendation

IF YOU CAN OBTAIN A LETTER OF RECOMMENDATION, YOU WILL HAVE something in writing to take with you as you continue your job search. Having something in writing from a business where you worked as a temporary employee could give you more credibility than only listing your staffing service as your place of work. Make sure you are accurate about having been a temporary worker at a particular company, and list the supervisor as your reference. If you list the personnel office of a company as your reference, that office may not be able to confirm your employment, because you are an employee of the staffing service, not of the places where you have worked as a temp.

What you want is credibility, and the way to get that is by asking the businesses where you work as a temp for a letter of recommendation. You want to get such a letter from the person who actually supervised you, not the personnel office. If you cannot get a letter of recommendation from some supervisors, ask them if you can list their names and phone numbers for reference phone calls. It never hurts to try, and it will prove you are serious about your job search.

Network

TAKE ADVANTAGE OF EVERY TEMPORARY JOB YOU GET AND NETWORK. At every place you work as a temp, ask people if they know of any full-time job openings. Ask for their help in getting interviews for jobs. Ask permission to list them as references in your resume as you send it to prospective employers.

What You Do Not Want to Do

YOU DO NOT WANT TO START TALKING ABOUT FULL-TIME WORK THE very first thing as you start a temp job. You are there to do a job, and that should be your first obligation. If you do not make a good first impression, no one will want to help you network your way into full-time work. In fact, if you make a bad impression, people who could have helped you will choose not to. Look what happened to Sandra.

Sandra wanted a full-time job in the entertainment industry. She had a degree in business with an emphasis in the recording industry. She had worked as an intern at a radio station in the city where her college was located. She had worked for no pay, something common for interns at her college, and she had worked in the mail room of the radio station, also common for interns.

Sandra decided to move to Los Angeles, where there were more companies in the recording business. She called several of the recording companies and learned they hired their employees through temp services and through internships. Since Sandra had already worked as an intern, she was not interested in doing so again. She asked the recording companies what staffing services they used and learned that most of the companies used the same three staffing services. One staffing service specialized in accounting, and the other two services did general office placement.

Sandra had taken two years of accounting and had trained on the computer programs that most accountants use. Since she wanted to work in the business office of a recording company, she decided to focus her energies on the staffing service that specialized in accounting.

At an interview with the accounting service, Sandra said she had chosen that service because she wanted a permanent job in the recording industry. She was introduced to Bill, who handled most of the temporary placement in the entertainment business.

Bill reviewed Sandra's application and her resume. He tested her on several accounting computer programs and told her he would call her after he checked her references.

Sandra called Bill the next day to see if he had a job for her. She knew Bill was busy and supervised lots of temps, so she did not want him to forget about her. Bill told her he was still looking and would be in touch when he had something for her. Sandra wrote Bill a thank-you note and called him again in three days.

Bill was impressed by Sandra's persistence, and her references had checked out. The staffing service Bill worked for had a temp-to-hire opening in a recording company. He told Sandra it was an entry-level position in the accounting office for someone to enter information on the computer. It was an important position, because the person entering the information needed to be accurate and concentrate on what he or she was doing. The recording company wanted to hire the temp full-time after 12 weeks if everything worked out.

Sandra was so excited. She told Bill she really wanted the opportunity. Bill warned her that this was a very important client to his service and he was risking a lot by sending her there. Sandra promised him he would not be sorry, and he gave her the job.

Sandra reported to work the next week and was introduced to her supervisor at the recording company, whose name was Jane. Jane was very glad to see her and said the department was behind schedule and needed someone who could really concentrate on what needed to be done and could stay focused.

Sandra had been at work about an hour when she left her desk and walked around to the various departments. She introduced herself to everyone she met, told them she was the new employee in the accounting office, asked lots of questions, and visited with many people. Jane was frantic when Sandra got back to her desk. It was only 10:00 A.M. and Jane thought Sandra might have left the building or walked off the job because she did not like it. Sandra assured Jane she wanted to stay and promised she would not leave her workstation except to go on scheduled break, to lunch, or to the bathroom. Jane thanked her and returned to her own work.

That afternoon, Sandra heard that one of the recording stars was in the building. The star was one of Sandra's favorites, so she left her desk and interrupted an important meeting to get the star's autograph. The star was nice enough to Sandra, but his manager was not impressed with Sandra, who had interrupted the meeting.

Jane's boss called her to complain about Sandra. When Bill called from the service to see how Sandra was working out, Jane said she did not think Sandra was going to be a match for the recording company. Her work was good, but she appeared to be too immature to concentrate on what she was there to do. Bill said he would replace Sandra. He also had to agree not to bill the business for any of the hours Sandra had worked as a temp. That meant the staffing service made zero money the day Sandra worked for them, but the staffing service had to pay Sandra for her hours.

Bill asked Sandra to come to his office at the staffing service at the end of her workday. He then told her she was fired from the staffing service and explained it was because of job performance. Sandra said she would do better the next time, and Bill said that might be true, but she should work with other services and not for his staffing service.

The recording company business was a small world, and the news about Sandra's job performance quickly spread from one company to another. When the other two services tried to place her, the recording companies refused, saying that they had heard about how Sandra behaved on her first temp job, and they did not want her to act the same way at their company. It was a tough lesson for Sandra to learn, and eventually she left Los Angeles and tried to start over at another location.

Read the Recruiting Ads

MAKE SURE YOU KEEP UP-TO-DATE WITH THE RECRUITING ADS WHERE you want to work. Do not assume just because you are registered with a staffing service that they will automatically call you for the job you really want. The personnel at staffing services get very busy and may occasionally overlook qualified people who are already registered with them. If you see or hear about something you want that your staffing service is advertising for, call the staffing service and tell them you want the job. The staffing service should appreciate your persistence and aggressiveness.

If the staffing service has you on a long-term job and you hear about another job that you would rather have, call the staffing service. Try to get the service to agree with you on a day that will be your last day on the long-term job so you can be placed on the job you really want. You should try to work with the service. If you can make it look good, the service should try to help you. You want to give the service time to find a replacement for you so that it looks good with the client where you are working.

If the staffing service will not work with you, suggest that you set the date you will leave the long-term job, and the service can then try to place you in the job you prefer. If the service still will not work with you, give notice and go work with another staffing service.

Continue to communicate on a regular basis with your staffing service or services. Do not let them put you on an assignment and forget about you. Remember that the staffing service would not have a product to sell if it were not for people like you who are willing to temp. Treat your contact at the staffing service like you would want to be treated. If you are not treated in a professional manner, quit and go work for someone else. If you have a consistent complaint about your staffing service, try speaking to someone other than your contact there. Ask for the president and see if he or she will help you before you quit. If you do quit, you will have to start over with another staffing service and build new relationships. Try to salvage your current relationships before you have to invest in building new relationships with a new staffing service.

Make Sure the Staffing Service Communicates Internally

MANY SERVICES ARE DIVIDED INTO TEMPORARY AND PERMANENT divisions. If you are working temp for the temporary division of the staffing service, the staff who place people on permanent jobs for that same service may not be aware of your qualifications and career goals.

If the staffing service you work for is divided into temporary and permanent divisions, make sure you have a contact in both divisions. If you accept a temporary job, communicate with your contact in the permanent division. Make sure the permanent division of a staffing service is sending out your resume for full-time jobs and schedules interviews for you while you temp for that service.

When you accept a temp job and you are looking for full-time work, make sure the temp job will allow you to interview for permanent jobs. That means the staffing service needs to arrange for your interviews during your lunchtime or early in the morning or late in the afternoon.

Unfortunately, some staffing services may tell you they will try to find a permanent job for you if you will temp for them while they look. Some services will tell you anything to get your skills for temp jobs. If you accept a temp job and you are not sent out for a permanent job within two weeks, you need to talk to your staffing service and decide how much of your time you want to spend with a service that does not send you out on interviews.

On the other hand, you could end up on a temp job that you like and that has the potential to go full-time. If you have flexibility you may want to consider temping for a while. If you do decide to, do not set any rigid deadlines for the staffing service you are temping for to find you a permanent job. Such deadlines may limit your opportunities for rewarding temporary assignments.

Conclusion

THE KEY TO WORKING WELL AS A TEMPORARY IS TO KNOW WHAT YOUR goals are. You need to know what money you must earn to meet your financial obligations as well as what kind of work you like. (You may not find out what you like until you have worked several different jobs.) Try to stay flexible. Flexibility will help you be successful in the world of temporary employment.

CHAPTER SEVENTEEN

Staffing Services in the 21st Century

PROFESSIONAL TEMPS WILL BE CALLED CONSULTANTS IN THE NEAR future. The image of the industry has changed, and some staffing services call temps consultants to reflect the respect that the corporate world now has for people who are a part of what has been called temporary employment.

The professional temp or consultant will go to staffing services that have something to offer. What will services offer? An attractive business mix.

Many companies have a list of vendors with whom they do business. Many are companies that are global and do business worldwide. They want to use staffing services that can send employees to their offices all over the world. So if your goal is to work for an international company or you want to travel, you need to select a staffing service that is global.

Search the Internet. The Web sites will tell you where the offices are for various staffing services. The offices will change daily with many of the services. A service that is in only a few states today may be as big as Adecco, Kelly, or Manpower through consolidations, mergers, and acquisitions in the near future.

The more professional technical temps a staffing service has working, the more jobs it will have to offer future temps. The more jobs a service has, the more temps it can attract. Therefore, services that have the most jobs will attract the most temps.

Services will become more and more competitive with benefits and training. The professional who decides to make temping a full-

STAFFING SERVICES IN THE 21ST CENTURY

time career will look for a staffing service that offers training. This is especially true for those who work in any area of information technology. And, almost every aspect of professional technical temping involves working with computers. Engineers, CADs, accountants, and even healthcare and research professionals all interact with computers. If someone is going to make a living as a full-time temp or consultant, that individual will look for a service that will help find state-of-the-art training.

The advantages of working with a large service are the opportunities for networking and the resources of a big company. These resources should include customizing the needs of the consultant and client, better pay, more benefits, global travel or work, and state-of-the-art training. If a service is smart, it will train the staff so that you, the temp, feel important and special every time you talk or interact with them. The service should develop a customized plan to meet your needs and at the same time customize a service delivery plan for the business it sends you to work for.

The disadvantages of working for a big service are the advantages of working for a small service. You may get more individual attention with a smaller service. But, you may feel like a big fish in a small pond. You need to be with a company that meets your needs. If you "think outside of the box," find a service that operates the same way. In other words, if you are open to working other than a 40-hour week, five days a week, between the hours of 8 A.M. and 5 P.M., look for a service that will match your needs.

A service that is proactive and plans ahead will be looking for ways to make sure its temps have the skills a client is looking for. You will know you have found the right service when you ask yourself, "Do I matter?" and the answer the service gives you is "Yes, you do and here are ways we can show you matter. We will offer you good pay, benefits, and training."

What skills will services be competitively recruiting for in the near future? Information technology skills will be in demand—anything that is a keyword-driven skill, from help desks to consulting that can pay from $30 to $250 an hour. Do you have a speciality in the information technology business? What have you fixed or accomplished? Get a list of information technology skills and research. The skills change daily.

Legal, accounting, and other skills that are technical in the fields of engineering, healthcare, and research will be needed. People who can work on projects will be in demand. Some generalists such as top management and CEOs may not find themselves working for staffing services but may instead be a part of the type of project work that companies like Arthur Andersen do; that is, where a company wants a solution to a problem and brings in a team of experts to offer suggestions on how to reorganize and to recommend who gets downsized or fired. Those people will come in, do their job, then go away. It remains to be seen whether the staffing industry will provide people to do these types of projects.

Temp Agency Resource Directory

I. INTERNATIONAL AND NATIONAL STAFFING SERVICES

GENERAL

AccuStaff
6440 Atlantic Boulevard
Jacksonville, FL 32211
1-800-526-5561
http://www.accustff.com

Adecco, Inc.
100 Redwood Shores Parkway
Redwood City, CA 94065
(415) 610-1000
Fax: (415) 610-1068
http://www.adecco.com

Interim Personnel
2050 Spectrum Boulevard
Fort Lauderdale, FL 33309
1-800-738-9370
http://www.interim.com

Kelly Services, Inc.
999 West Big Beaver Road
Troy, MI 48084
(248) 362-4444
Fax: (248) 244-4154
http://www.kellyservices.com

Manpower Inc.
P.O. Box 2053
5301 North Ironwood Road
Milwaukee, WI 53201-2053
(414) 961-1000
Fax: (414) 961-2124
http://www.manpower.com

Norrell Corporation
3535 Piedmont Road, NE
Atlanta, GA 30305
(404) 240-3000
Fax: (404) 240-3029
http://www.norrell.com

Olsten Corporation
175 Broad Hollow Road
Melville, NY 11747
(516) 844-7800, ext. 7241
Fax: (516) 844-7077
http://www.olsten.com

Robert Half International, Inc.
2884 Sand Hill Road
Menlo Park, CA 94025
(415) 234-6000
http://www.rhii.com

Snelling Personnel Services
Suite 700
12801 North Central Expressway
Dallas, TX 75243
(214) 239-7575
Fax: (214) 239-6881

StaffMark
302 East Millsap Road
Fayetteville, AR 72703
(501) 973-6000
Fax: (501) 973-6019
http://www.staffmark.com

ACCOUNTING AND FINANCE

Accountants on Call
A Division of Adecco Services, Inc.
525 Fifth Avenue
Suite 1200
New York, NY 10017
(212) 682-5900
http://www.aocnet.com/aoc

Accountemps—Robert Half
2884 Sand Hill Road
Menlo Park, CA 94025
1-800-803-8367
http://www.accountemps.com

BUSINESS

Marshall Consultants
Freelance Communicators
360 East 65th Street, Penthouse B
New York, NY 10021
(212) 628-8400
http://www.marshallconsultants.com
Corporate communications, public
relations, advertising, investor
relations, and marketing

MB Inc. Executive Search
505 Fifth Avenue
New York, NY 10017
(212) 661-4937
http://www.mbincexec.com
Marketing, sales, finance, and
general management executives for
assignments

Mortgage Bankers' Consultants
2805 Allen Street
Columbus Square, Suite 217
Dallas, TX 75204
1-800-736-work
http://www.mbctemps.com
Mortgage banking professionals
and executives for national
assignments

Paladin Companies Inc.
11990 San Vincente Boulevard
Suite 350
Los Angeles, CA 90049
(310) 826-6222
http://www.paladinstaff.com
Advertising, marketing, public
relations, creative specialists

*Princeton Entrepreneurial Resources
  Inc.*
P.O. Box 2051
Princeton, NJ 08543
(609) 243-0010
http://www.per-inc.com
Senior executives in all functional
areas

LEGAL

The Affiliates
A Division of Robert Half
  International
Corporate Headquarters
1901 Avenue of the Stars
Suite 350
Los Angeles, CA 90067-6006
(310) 557-2666
http://www.affiliates.com
Other offices in Chicago, IL, Irvine,
CA, Los Angeles, CA, Palo Alto,
CA, San Francisco, CA, Seattle,
WA, Washington, DC

Amicus Legal Staffing, Inc.
Corporate Headquarters
Signature Center
Suite 425
1900 Church Street
Nashville, TN 37203
1-800-898-5118
http://www.amicus-staffing.com
Other offices in Austin, TX,
Birmingham, AL, Charlotte, NC,
Dallas, TX, Jackson, MS, Knoxville,
TN, Memphis, TN, New Orleans,
LA

Special Counsel
A Division of Accustaff
Corporate Headquarters
16 South Calvert Street
Suite 501
Baltimore, MD 21202
1-800-737-3436
http://www.accustaff.com

Serving Atlanta, GA, Baltimore,
MD, Boston, MA, Charlotte, NC,
Chicago, IL, Cleveland, OH, Dallas,
TX, Denver, CO, Houston, TX,
Jacksonville, FL, Los Angeles, CA,
Miami, FL, New York, NY, Phoenix,
AR, Sacramento, CA, San
Francisco, CA, Santa Clara, CA,
Seattle, WA, Washington, DC

The Wallace Law Registry
A Subsidiary of Kelly Services
43 Woodland Street, Suite 400
Hartford, CT 06105
1-800-248-4LAW
http://www.kellyservices.com
Offices in Atlanta, GA, Boston,
  MA, Chicago, IL, Detroit, MI,
  Hartford, CT, Los Angeles, CA,
  Miami, FL, Minneapolis, MN,
  Newark, NJ, Norfolk, VA,
  Philadelphia, PA, San Francisco,
  CA, Stamford, CT, Washington,
  DC

MEDICAL

*Gregory & Gregory Medical
  Staffing*
19 West 44th Street
New York, NY 10036
(212) 944-2888

Maxwell Medical Staffing
82221 East 63rd Place
Tulsa, OK 74133
(918) 459-2955
Medical placement, front and back
office

MRIC
1040–1140 West Pender Street
Vancouver, British Columbia
    V64EG1
1-800-668-6742
http://www.mric.com
Medical recruiters

Starmed Health Personnel, Inc.
14 Perimeter Center East
Suite 1425
Atlanta, GA 30346
(770) 913-9071

SCIENTIFIC

Kelly Scientific Resources
A Division of Kelly Services
999 West Big Beaver Road
Troy, MI 48084
1-800-KELLY62
http://www.kellyservices.com
25 branch offices in the U.S. and
    Canada

TECHNICAL

AlternaStaff
Division of Fortune Franchise
    Corporation
1155 Avenue of the Americas
New York, NY 10036
1-800-886-7839
http://www.fpcweb.com.franchise
Executives, middle managers, and
technical professionals in all
industries

Baker Street Group, Inc.
1250 Wood Branch Park
Suite 400
Houston, TX 77079
(281) 870-8707
Professional technical

Career Marketing Associates Inc.
7100 East Belleview Avenue
Suite 102
Greenwood Village, CO 80111
(303) 779-8890
http://www.cmagroup.com
Technical—engineering, computer
hardware and software,
communications, environmental,
and regulatory

Clinical Trials Support Services
P.O. Box 14289
Research Triangle Park, NC 27709
(919) 941-0844
Research

CT Engineering Corporation
2221 Rosecrans Avenue
Suite 131
El Segundo, CA 90245
(310) 643-8333
http://www.cteng.com
High-tech professionals—engineers,
scientists, computer programmers,
and software developers serving
Southern California

DP Pros
2639 Ramada Road
Burlington, NC 27215
(910) 222-8030
Professional technical

Expert Business Systems, Inc.
500 Grapevine Highway
Suite 224
Hurst, TX 77079
(817) 514-7373
Computer information
technology

Flexible Technologies
200 North Copperwood Court
Muncie, IN 47304
(317) 741-0526
http://www.flexgrp.com
General recruiters, professional and
technical

Global Dynamics, Inc.
1350 Treat Boulevard, Suite 350
Walnut Creek, CA 94596
(510) 946-0601
http://www.globaldynamics.com
Computer information technology

InterExec. From MRI
Division of Management Recruiters
    International, Inc.
200 Public Square, 31st Floor
Cleveland, OH 44114
1-800-875-4000
http://www.mrinet.com
Professional, technical, and
management

Joulé Technical Staffing Inc.
1235 Route 1 South
Edison, NJ 08837
1-800-382-0382
http://www.jouleinc.com
Design, drafting, engineering, and
research assistants

Kelly Technical Services
A Division of Kelly Services
999 West Big Beaver Road
Troy, MI 48084
(248) 362-4444
http://www.kellyservices.com
More than 50 branches in the U.S.
    and Canada

The Kleven Group, Inc.
One Cranberry Hill
Lexington, MA 02173
(617) 861-1029
Professional technical

Lindenberg & Associates, Inc.
701 Emerson Road
Suite 300
St. Louis, MO 63141
1-800-209-9852
Professional technical

*Maxwell Sumner Ray Technical
    Services*
4775 South Harvard, Suite D
Tulsa, OK 74135
(918) 742-9760
http://www.sumray@ionet.com
Professional technical

On Assignment
26651 West Agoura Road
Calabasas, CA 91302
(818) 878-7900
http://www.assignment.com
Scientists and other professional
technical skills

On Call Technical Services
3850 North Grant Avenue
Suite 100
Loveland, CO 80538
(970) 667-6222
http://www.stafftech.com

Sterling Human Resource Company
3410 East University Drive,
    #300
Phoenix, AZ 85034
(602) 470-8000
Professional technical

Strategic Sourcing
6525 Morrison Boulevard
Suite 503
Charlotte, NC 28211
1-800-371-8367

Technology Source
12400 Olive Boulevard, Suite 350
St. Louis, MO 63141
(314) 878-6903
http://www.techsourc.com
Computer information
   technology

Temp Technology, Inc.
4900 WE Griffith Drive,
   Suite 163
Beaverton, OR 97005
(503) 626-6378
Professional technical

Tom Bain Personnel
5100 Maryland Way
Center Court Building, Suite 290
Brentwood, TN 37027
(615) 371-1400
healthcare, information technology,
accounting, engineering, human
resources

The Whitaker Companies Inc.
820 Gessner, Suite 1400
Houston, TX 77024
(713) 465-1500
http://www.whitakercos.com
Temporary physicians and medical
professionals—physician's assistants,
nurse practitioners, anesthetists;
information technology consultants,
contract engineers, legal

II. LOCAL TEMP SERVICES

ALABAMA

Huntsville
Accent' Human Resources, Inc.
Suite 5
4820 University Drive
Huntsville, AL 35816
(205) 895-0505
Fax: (205) 895-0785

Mobile
*ACO Employment & Information
   Services*
Suite 100
9 Dauphin Street
Mobile, AL 36602
(334) 433-7788
Fax: (334) 433-7789

ALASKA

Anchorage
Elite Temporaries
Suite 200
1113 West Fireweed Lane
Anchorage, AK 90503-1704
(907) 276-8367
Fax: (907) 276-5172

Wasilla
MECA Employment Connection
Suite 592
1830 East Park Highway
Wasilla, AK 99634
(907) 376-6322
Fax: (907) 373-6322

ARIZONA

Mesa

Advanced Labor
1201 South Alma School Road
Mesa, AZ 85210
(602) 833-3655
Fax: (602) 833-3667

*AllHealth Medical Personnel
   Specialists*
Suite 119
777 West Southern Avenue
Mesa, AZ 85021
(602) 649-9260
Fax: (602) 649-9578

Phoenix

*Accent' Human Resource
   Specialists*
Suite 145
2930 East Camelback Road
Phoenix, AZ 85016
(602) 955-2222
Fax: (602) 955-0914

Yuma

A.C.E. Personnel Services
Suite B
1020 South Fourth Avenue
Yuma, AZ 85364
(602) 782-1683
Fax: (602) 782-9499

ACME Temporary Services
550 East 32nd Street, Suite 2
Yuma, AZ 85365
(520) 344-8367
Fax: (520) 344-8282

ARKANSAS

Hot Springs

Prostaff, a Division of StaffMark
3810 Central Avenue, Suite A
Hot Springs, AR 71913
(501) 525-4443
Fax: (501) 525-4486

Little Rock

Prostaff, a Division of StaffMark
2024 Arkansas Valley Drive
Little Rock, AR 72212
(501) 225-5050
Fax: (501) 225-2788

Springdale

A.S.A.P. Services, Inc.
P.O. Box 1683
Springdale, AR 72765-1683
(501) 750-2727
Fax: (501) 750-2748

CALIFORNIA

Alamo

Advantage Personnel Services
P.O. Box 800
Alamo, CA 94507-0800
(510) 831-9000

Bell

Affiliated Temporary Service
P.O. Box 124
Bell, CA 90201-0013
(213) 771-1383
Fax: (213) 771-8300

Burlingame
Accountants Inc.
Suite 400
111 Anza Boulevard
Burlingame, CA 94010-1932
(415) 579-1111
Fax: (415) 579-1927

Covina
Advantage Staffing, Inc.
Suite 31
750 Terrado Plaza
Covina, CA 91723
(818) 859-2366
Fax: (818) 915-0330

Grand Terrace
A MacRey Corporation
Suite J
12210 Michigan Avenue
Grand Terrace, CA 92313
(909) 825-7010
Fax: (909) 825-7055

La Mirada
All Temporaries, Inc.
Suite 106
14752 Beach Boulevard
La Mirada, CA 90638
(714) 562-8550
Fax: (714) 562-8556

Los Angeles
Accountants Overload
Suite #1400
10990 Wilshire Boulevard
Los Angeles, CA 90024
(310) 478-8883
Fax: (310) 478-9591

Menlo Park
Accountemps Service of Robert Half
International
2884 Sand Hill Road
Menlo Park, CA 94025
(415) 854-9700
Fax: (415) 854-9735

Redwood City
Adia Services, Inc.
100 Redwood Shores Parkway
Redwood City, CA 94065
(415) 610-1000
Fax: (415) 610-1068

San Diego
Abcow Services, Inc.
Suite 125
2525 Camino del Rio South
San Diego, CA 92108
(619) 291-7000
Fax: (619) 291-7171

San Francisco
Alan J. Blair Personnel Services
Suite 200
625 Market Street
San Francisco, CA 94105
(415) 243-0440
Fax: (415) 394-8673

Tustin
Abigail Abbott Staffing Services, Inc.
660 West First Street
Tustin, CA 92680
(714) 731-7711
Fax: (714) 731-6570

Vernon
Alternative Labor Source, Inc.
3228 East 50th Street
Vernon, CA 90058
(213) 588-1114
Fax: (213) 581-0584

COLORADO

Boulder
Brewer/OnCall, a Division of StaffMark
1680 30th Street
Boulder, CO 80301
(303) 444-4558
Fax: (303) 443-7940

Colorado Springs
ADDSTAFF, Inc.
2118 Hollowbrook Drive
Colorado Springs, CO 80918
(719) 528-8888
Fax: (719) 528-8890

Englewood
Accounting Quest
Suite 514
5660 Greenwood Plaza Boulevard
Englewood, CO 80111
(303) 773-6100
Fax: (303) 773-9225

Loveland
*Brewer/OnCall, a Division of
    StaffMark*
118 East 29th Street
Suite F
Loveland, CO 80538
(970) 667-6222
Fax: (970) 667-8966

Westminster
*Kelly Scientific Resources—Western
    Region*
Sheridan Park 2, Suite 105
8753 Yates Drive
Westminister, CO 80030-6947
(303) 427-4140
Fax (303) 427-4875

CONNECTICUT

New Hartford
Alternative Employment
Suite 3
100 Business Park Drive
New Hartford, CT 06057
(860) 489-1463
Fax: (860) 489-1534

Norwalk
Admiral Temps
37 North Avenue
Norwalk, CT 06851
(203) 847-9600
Fax: (203) 846-8333

Stamford
Advantage L.P.
4th Floor
1055 Washington Boulevard
Stamford, CT 06901
(203) 352-5936
Fax: (203) 323-1431

DELAWARE

Wilmington
Bernard Personnel Consultants
534 Greenhill Avenue
Wilmington, DE 19805
(302) 655-4491
Fax: (302) 655-4401

Caldwell Staffing Services
8 South DuPont Road
Wilmington, DE 19805
(302) 655-9500
Fax: (302) 655-7228

Temps Work, Inc.
Suite 101
1200 Pennsylvania Avenue
Wilmington, DE 19086
(302) 777-5555
Fax: (302) 777-5554

DISTRICT OF COLUMBIA

Best Temporaries, Inc.
Suite 801
1101 Connecticut Avenue NW
Washington, DC 20036
(202) 293-7333
Fax: (202) 861-0297

CompuStaff Personnel
Suite 700 North
601 Pennsylvania Avenue NW
Washington, DC 20004
(202) 554-3644
Fax: (202) 554-3699

FLORIDA

Clearwater
Abilities, Inc. of Florida
2735 Whitney Road
Clearwater, FL 34620
(813) 538-7370, ext. 355
Fax: (813) 538-7387

Ablest Service Corporation
810 North Belcher Road
Clearwater, FL 34625
(813) 461-5656
Fax: (813) 447-1146

A Workable Company Inc.
Suite 812
13923 Icot Boulevard
Clearwater, FL 34620
(813) 530-5575
Fax: (813) 530-1749

Coral Gables
AdStaff Personnel Services, Inc.
273 Alhambra Circle
Coral Gables, FL 33143
(305) 443-2122
Fax: (305) 443-6128

Hollywood
All Medical Personnel
Suite 100
2501 Hollywood Boulevard
Hollywood, FL 33020
(954) 927-2800
Fax: (954) 923-8721

Jacksonville
AccuStaff Inc.
6440 Atlantic Boulevard
Jacksonville, FL 32211
(904) 725-5574
Fax: (904) 725-8513

Miami
Ambiance Personnel, Inc.
Suite 125
7990 SW 117 Avenue
Miami, FL 33183-3845
(305) 274-7419
Fax: (305) 598-8071

Pinellas Park
Alternative Temps
4326 Park Boulevard
Pinellas Park, FL 34665
(813) 547-8367
Fax: (813) 547-8371

Tampa
ACA International
14130 McCormick Drive
Tampa, FL 33626
(813) 855-9411
Fax: (813) 854-3359

Accord Personnel Services
Suite 400
4040 West Waters Avenue
Tampa, FL 33614
(813) 887-3290
Fax: (813) 887-5340

A. J. O'Neal & Associates, Inc.
109-A Falkenburg Road
Tampa, FL 33619-9704
(813) 654-4199
Fax: (813) 654-7726

GEORGIA

Atlanta
Access Personnel Services, Inc.
Suite 420
200 Galleria Parkway
Atlanta, GA 30339
(770) 988-8484
Fax: (770) 988-8522

Accounting Alternatives
Suite 550
35 Glenlake Parkway
Atlanta, GA 30328
(404) 671-9647
Fax: (404) 676-1341

All Medical Personnel
Suite 104B
1961 North Druid Hills Road
Atlanta, GA 30329
(404) 320-9125
Fax: (404) 320-9182

A One Service Personnel
Suite 157
1718 Peachtree Street
Atlanta, GA 30309
(404) 885-9675
Fax: (404) 885-9666

Brewer/Caldwell, a Division of
StaffMark
200 Galleria Parkway
Suite 905
Atlanta, GA 30339
(770) 955-1767
Fax: (770) 955-0114

Marietta
Ad Options, Inc.
P.O. Box 7778
Marietta, GA 30065
(770) 514-7778
Fax: (770) 919-2254

Roswell/Cumming
Brewer/Caldwell, a Division of
StaffMark
101 Meadow Drive
Suite G
Cumming, GA 30130
(770) 886-7457
Fax: (770) 886-7364

Tucker
Alternative Staffing, Inc.
Building 5, Suite 21
2179 North Lake Parkway
Tucker, GA 30084
(404) 908-8710
Fax: (404) 908-1836

Tyrone
AAA Staffing, Inc.
P.O. Box 817
Tyrone, GA 30290
(770) 254-8766
Fax: (770) 254-0974

HAWAII

Honolulu
ALTRES Staffing
Suite 110
711 Kapiolani Boulevard
Honolulu, HI 96813
(808) 591-4950
Fax: (808) 591-1711

IDAHO

Meridian
A.E.S. Inc. An Employment Source
P.O. Box 567
Meridian, ID 83680
(208) 887-7740
Fax: (208) 888-7872

ILLINOIS

Chicago
ABLE's Pool of Temporaries
Suite 802
180 North Wabash
Chicago, IL 60601
(312) 580-1490
Fax: (312) 580-0348

Accurate Recruiting, Inc.
Suite 2007
200 West Adams Street
Chicago, IL 60606
(312) 357-2500
Fax: (312) 630-1165

Ad Temps, Inc.
Suite 500
311 West Superior Street
Chicago, IL 60610
(312) 751-0090
Fax: (312) 751-0089

AIC Temporary Service
Suite 1B
1807 West Sunnyside
Chicago, IL 60640-5803
(312) 292-8657
Fax: (312) 292-8663

AltraStaff Personnel Services, Inc.
Suite 100
5331 West Ainslie Street
Chicago, IL 60630
(312) 777-3330
Fax: (312) 777-6459

A Personnel Commitment
208 South LaSalle Street
Chicago, IL 60604-1004
(800) GET-A-JOB
Fax: (312) 251-5154

Franklin Park
Alpha Temporary Service
9611 West Grand Avenue
Franklin Park, IL 60131
(708) 455-3100
Fax: (708) 455-2101

Lansing
ABLE Temps, Inc.
Suite E-1
2533 Bernice Road
Lansing, IL 60438
(708) 895-9200
Fax: (708) 895-3832

Lincolnshire
Alternative Resources Corporation
Suite 100
75 Tri-State International
Lincolnshire, IL 60069
(708) 317-1000
Fax: (708) 317-1008

Long Grove

AllStaff Services
Suite B
3880 Salem Lake Drive
Long Grove, IL 60047
(708) 726-0726
Fax: (708) 540-9988

Springfield

Alice Campbell Temporaries
Suite D
2121 West White Oaks Drive
Springfield, IL 62704
(217) 793-5522
Fax: (217) 793-5527

INDIANA

Terre Haute

21st Century Personnel
Suite 214
22 North 5th Street
Terre Haute, IN 47807
(812) 232-3806
Fax: (812) 235-3269

IOWA

Bettendorf

All Staff, Inc.
Suite 240 South
2435 Kimberly Road
Bettendorf, IA 52722
(319) 359-6884
Fax: (319) 355-0118

KANSAS

Overland Park

Century Personnel
5300 College Boulevard
Overland Park, KS 66211
(913) 451-2043

Encore Temporary Services
8607 College Boulevard
Overland Park, KS 66210
(913) 491-TEMP

Excel Personnel Services
7300 West 110th Street, Suite 150
Overland Park, KS 66210
(913) 345-0004
Fax: (913) 491-3577

Wichita

Total Temporary Services
P.O. Box 818
127 South Hydraulic
Wichita, KS 67201-0818
(316) 267-2561
Fax: (316) 267-3121

KENTUCKY

Lexington

Judy's Temporaries, Inc.
3070 Harrodsburg Road, Suite 130
Lexington, KY 40503
(606) 223-5005
Fax: (606) 223-3103

Louisville

Ahead Staffing, Inc.
2207 Heather Lane
Louisville, KY 40218
(502) 485-1000
Fax: (502) 485-0801

LOUISIANA

Baton Rouge

Advantage Personnel, Inc.
11224 Boardwalk, Suite E-1-1
Baton Rouge, LA 70816-8345
(504) 273-8900
Fax: (504) 273-8909

Luling
AM-PM Temporary Services
13505 River Road
Luling, LA 70070
(504) 785-6857
Fax: (504) 785-6462

New Orleans
Brooke Staffing Companies
701 Poydras Street
New Orleans, LA 70139-0001
(504) 581-3181
Fax: (504) 581-3189

MAINE

Bangor
Downeast Temporary Services
P.O. Box 603
Bangor, ME 04402-0603
(207) 947-7541
Fax: (207) 947-6704

Brooks
@Work JAMB Personnel Service, Inc.
P.O. Box 96
Corner of Routes 139 & 7
Brooks, ME 04921-0096
(207) 722-3568
Fax: (207) 722-3745

Portland
Springborn Staffing Services, Inc.
130 Middleton Street
Portland, ME 04101
(207) 761-8367
Fax: (207) 775-2359

MARYLAND

Baltimore
Able Temporaries
Suite 700
2 North Charles Street
Baltimore, MD 21201
(410) 685-8189
Fax: (410) 625-6177

AdNet/AccountNet, Inc.
Suite 402
210 East Lombard Street
Baltimore, MD 21202
(410) 659-0002
Fax: (410) 752-8640

*Advanced Resource Management
    Systems*
Suite 107
1900 East Northern Parkway
Baltimore, MD 21239
(410) 323-8900
Fax: (410) 323-8942

A. J. Burton Group, Inc.
Suite 2220
120 East Baltimore Street
Baltimore, MD 21202
(410) 752-5244
Fax: (410) 752-5924

LaVale
ACT Personnel Service, Inc.
P.O. Box 3326
LaVale, MD 21504
(301) 724-1035
Fax: (301) 724-4550

Salisbury

AAA Employment Agency, Inc.
Suite A
1501 Edgemore Avenue
Salisbury, MD 21801
(410) 546-5955
Fax: (410) 548-5312

MASSACHUSETTS

Boston

Alternative Solutions, Inc.
P.O. Box 740
396 Commonwealth Avenue
Boston, MA 02117-0740
(617) 262-4900
Fax: (617) 262·6217

Fall River

Able Associates
1504 Pleasant Street
Fall River, MA 02723-1900
(508) 673-3979
Fax: (508) 673-0978

Gloucester

AlternaTemps, Inc.
35 Middle Street
Gloucester, MA 01930
(508) 283-4909
Fax: (508) 768-7121

Norton

The Alpha Group
175 Mansfield Avenue
Norton, MA 02766
(508) 285-8500

Worcester

Accurate Staffing Services, Inc.
Suite 830
390 Main Street
Worcester, MA 01608
(508) 799-9599
Fax: (508) 798-2731

MICHIGAN

Bay City

Heartland Health Care
401 Center Avenue
Bay City, MI 48707-2276
(517) 893-4801
Fax: (517) 893-4945

Grand Rapids

Account Ability Now
1149 Bridgewater Place
Grand Rapids, MI 49501
(616) 235-1149
Fax: (616) 235-1148

1st Agency Professionals
511 Wilson NW
Grand Rapids, MI 49504
(616) 791-4260
Fax: (616) 791-7039

Lansing

Advance Employment
4407 West St. Joseph Highway
Lansing, MI 48917
(517) 321-5700
Fax: (517) 321-6077

Livonia

Accountants Connection, Inc.
Suite 100
32540 Schoolcraft Road
Livonia, MI 48150
(313) 513-7800
Fax: (313) 513-7805

Midland
Allied Technical Services
2957 Venture Drive
Midland, MI 48640
(517) 832-9063
Fax: (517) 832-9069

Monroe
Advance Temporary Services, Inc.
36 East Front Street
Monroe, MI 48161
(313) 457-0056
Fax: (313) 457-0362

Southfield
Accountants One, Inc.
Suite 516
24901 Northwestern Highway
Southfield, MI 48075
(810) 354-2410
Fax: (810) 354-2017

Troy
Alternative Staff, Inc.
1000 John Road, Suite 102
Troy, MI 48083-5849
(810) 589-3830
Fax: (810) 589-3239

Kelly Scientific Resources—Central Region
999 West Big Beaver Road
Troy, MI 48084
(248) 244-4355
Fax: (248) 244-5440

Wayne
Add-A-Tech, Inc.
3139 South Wayne Road
Wayne, MI 48184-1220
(800) 823-2722
Fax: (313) 722-7006

MINNESOTA

Bloomington
Alternative Staffing, Inc.
Suite 570
8120 Penn Avenue South
Bloomington, MN 55431-1326
(612) 888-6077
Fax: (612) 888-6153

1st Street Northwest, Inc.
Suite 112
8030 Cedar Avenue South
Bloomington, MN 55425
(612) 854-7000
Fax: (612) 854-4533

Maplewood
ADDON Temporary Services, Inc.
Suite 50
255 East Roselawn Avenue
Maplewood, MN 55117
(612) 488-1000
Fax: (612) 488-9585

St. Paul
A Window of Opportunity
Suite 3294
1565 Cliff Road
St. Paul, MN 55122
(612) 894-7906
Fax: (612) 452-4037

MISSISSIPPI

Jackson
TemPro, Inc.
Suite 500
1510 North State
Jackson, MS 39202
(601) 355-7000
Fax: (601) 353-5014

MISSOURI

Columbia
Personnel Advantage
2116 Nelwood Drive
Columbia, MO 65202-3645
(314) 474-1550
Fax: (314) 474-8575

St. Louis
Linde Group Temporaries of St. Louis, Inc.
11325 Concord Village Avenue
St. Louis, MO 63123
(314) 842-5522

MONTANA

Billings
The Temporary Connection
Suite 22
848 Main Street
Billings, MT 59105
(406) 252-8430
Fax: (406) 252-1599

NEBRASKA

Lincoln
Advantage Personnel, Inc.
Suite 100
630 North Cotner Boulevard
Lincoln, NE 68505
(402) 466-4994
Fax: (402) 466-6397

NEVADA

Las Vegas
Allen Temporary Staffing
Suite 118
1700 East Desert Inn Road
Las Vegas, NV 89109
(702) 731-5734
Fax: (702) 731-2066

NEW HAMPSHIRE

Portsmouth
Able 1 Staffing Services, Inc.
126 Daniel Street
Portsmouth, NH 03801
(603) 436-1151
Fax: (603) 436-0285

Rye
Allstaff
300 Lafayette Road
Rye, NH 03870
(603) 964-1780
Fax: (603) 964-1657

NEW JERSEY

Edison
ALTCO Temporary Services
100 Menlo Park
Edison, NJ 08837
(908) 549-6100
Fax: (908) 549-6105

Park Ridge
Aides/Temporary Employment, Inc.
52 Park Avenue
Park Ridge, NJ 07656
(201) 391-1550
Fax: (201) 391-0670

Piscataway

*Kelly Scientific Resources—Eastern
Region*
242 Old New Brunswick Road
Suitte 140
Piscataway, NJ 08854-3754
(732) 981-1399
Fax: (732) 981-1377

NEW MEXICO

Albuquerque

Advantage Staffing Resources
1334 Wyoming Boulevard NE
Albuquerque, NM 87112
(505) 292-3451
Fax: (505) 292-0079

Monticello

Action-Plus Temporary Service
P.O. Box 898
141 East Broadway
Monticello, NM 55362
(612) 395-4005
Fax: (612) 295-6240

NEW YORK

New York

Accountants & Auditors Temporaries
Suite 603
310 Madison Avenue
New York, NY 10017
(212) 687-5656
Fax: (212) 983-3538

AlternaStaff Services, Inc.
15th Floor
1155 Avenue of the Americas
New York, NY 10036
(212) 302-1141
Fax: (212) 302-2422

Smithtown

A.S.A.P. Temporaries
765 Nesconset Highway
Smithtown, NY 11787
(516) 265-3800
Fax: (516) 265-3853

NORTH CAROLINA

Charlotte

*First Choice, a Division of
StaffMark*
6600 In East W.T. Harris
Boulevard
Charlotte, NC 28215
(704) 537-4700
Fax: (704) 537-6333

Durham

*The Blethen Group, a Division of
StaffMark*
3505 University Drive
Durham, NC 27707
(919) 493-8367
Fax: (919) 490-1650

Gastonia

ABE-L Personnel
P.O. Box 292
1508 South York Road
Gastonia, NC 28052
(704) 864-1224
Fax: (704) 864-1075

Wilson

*Action Temporaries Management
Company Inc.*
210 North Tarboro Street
Wilson, NC 27893
(919) 237-3717
Fax: (919) 237-3720

NORTH DAKOTA

Fargo
Preferred Temporary Services
Suite 108
1351 Page Drive
Fargo, ND 58103
(701) 293-9349
Fax: (701) 293-0281

OHIO

Beachwood
All Star Temporary Services, Inc.
Suite 260
21625 Chagrin Boulevard
Beachwood, OH 44122
(216) 991-7827
Fax: (216) 991-3704

Cincinnati
*ADOW Personnel/Techtalent-
    Staffmatch-Executeam*
Suite 1020
36 East Fourth Street
Cincinnati, OH 45202-3816
(513) 721-2369
Fax: (513) 721-3724

Cleveland
ABT Staffing Division of AB Temps
1127 Euclid Avenue
Cleveland, OH 44115
(216) 771-8367
Fax: (216) 566-1536

Columbus
Abby Lane/Dana Temporaries, Inc.
196 East State Street
Columbus, OH 43215
(614) 621-3262
Fax: (614) 621-3312

A-Plus Personnel Services, Inc.
145 East Rich Street
Columbus, OH 43215
(614) 238-0665
Fax: (614) 238-0673

Strongsville
All All-American Temps, Inc.
13477 Prospect Road, Suite 103 B
Strongsville, OH 44136
(216) 572-0211
Fax: (216) 572-1041

OKLAHOMA

Tulsa
Accounting Principals
1202 South Boulder
Tulsa, OK 74119-2828
(918) 584-3300
Fax: (918) 584-3800

Maxwell, a Division of StaffMark
4775 South Harvard, Suite E
Tulsa, OK 74135
(918) 744-8367

OREGON

Eugene
SelecTemp Corporation
2131 Centennial Plaza
Eugene, OR 97401
(503) 344-6200
Fax: (503) 686-2130

Portland
Boly/Welch Temporary Services
9th Floor
806 SW Broadway
Portland, OR 97205
(503) 242-1300
Fax: (503) 323-9087

221

PENNSYLVANIA

Allentown
Allied Temporary Services
2nd Floor
667 Union Boulevard
Allentown, PA 18103
(610) 821-0220
Fax: (610) 821-8808

Dickson City
Action Personnel Services
1622 Main Street
Dickson City, PA 18447
(717) 383-0243
Fax: (717) 383-2565

Erie
All Seasons Placement
3618 West 12th Street
Erie, PA 16505
(814) 838-2743

King of Prussia
Accounting Pros
Suite 205
1060 First Avenue
King of Prussia, PA 19406
(610) 337-4800
Fax: (610) 337-9466

Pittsburgh
Allegheny Personnel Services
Suite 205, Two PNC Plaza
620 Liberty Avenue
Pittsburgh, PA 15222
(412) 391-2044

PUERTO RICO

Santurce
Pro-Tempo, Inc.
Suite 508
Cond. San Martin
Santurce, PR 00909
(809) 723-8159
Fax: (809) 725-9587

RHODE ISLAND

Providence
Employment USA, Inc.
705 Westminster Street
Providence, RI 02903
(401) 351-5590
Fax: (401) 331-1732

Job Link, Inc.
674 Elmwood Avenue
Providence, RI 02907-3353
(401) 941-3240, ext. 123
Fax: (401) 467-4414

SOUTH CAROLINA

Charleston
Charles Foster Staffing
Suite 240
7301 Rivers Avenue
Charleston, SC 29406
(803) 572-8100
Fax: (803) 572-3574

Columbia
U.S. Personnel, Inc.
Suite 2250
2000 Center Point Drive
Columbia, SC 29210
(803) 551-2636
Fax: (803) 551-2635

Rock Hill

First Choice, a Division of StaffMark
1630 Ebenezer Road
Rock Hill, SC 29732
(803) 324-2425
Fax: (803) 329-5348

SOUTH DAKOTA

Sioux Falls
Action Temporary & Personnel, Inc.
1010 West 41st Street
Sioux Falls, SD 57105
(605) 338-6465
Fax: (605) 338-6469

TENNESSEE

Germantown/Memphis
*Accountants & Bookkeepers
Personnel, Inc.*
P.O. Box 38304
Germantown, TN 38183
(901) 755-6444
Fax: (901) 755-2567

Memphis
Access Personnel, Inc.
Suite 106
280 Hernando Street
Memphis, TN 38126
(901) 529-8384
Fax: (901) 529-8314

Advance Personnel Service, Inc.
Suite 1
5090 Millbranch
Memphis, TN 38116-7239
(901) 332-0291
Fax: (901) 398-7185

Nashville
Wood Personnel Services
Professional Search Division
1321 Murfreesboro Road
Suite 140
Nashville, TN 37217
(615) 399-0019
Fax: (615) 377-3435

TEXAS

Arlington
Ad-a-Staff, Inc.
Suite 213
711 East Lamar Boulevard
Arlington, TX 76011
(817) 459-1227
Fax: (817) 459-0230

Bellaire
Access Information Associates, Inc.
Suite 140
4710 Bellaire Boulevard
Bellaire, TX 77401-4505
(713) 664-4357
Fax: (713) 664-4825

Dallas
Absolutely Professional Temps
13355 Noel Road
Dallas, TX 75240
(214) 661-1500
Fax: (214) 661-1309

Euless
1st Odyssey Group
310 South Industrial Boulevard
Euless, TX 76040
(817) 267-6090
Fax: (817) 868-1731

UTAH

Salt Lake City
SOS Staffing Services
1415 South Main
Salt Lake City, UT 84115
(801) 484-4400
Fax: (801) 486-3131

Wasatch Temporary Services
Suite 100
845 East 4800 South
Salt Lake City, UT 84107-5040
(801) 268-3990
Fax: (801) 268-3626

VERMONT

Brattleboro
GFI Professional Staffing Services
P.O. Box 8144
Brattleboro, VT 05304
(802) 257-1146

Harmon Personnel Services, Inc.
50 Elliott Street
Brattleboro, VT 05301
(802) 254-8639

Manchester Center
Heritage Personnel Services, Inc.
P.O. Box 1284
Manchester Center, VT 05255
(802) 362-5613

South Burlington
Norrell Services
1233 Shelburne Road
Suite 300
South Burlington, VT 05403
(802) 864-5900

Olsten Staffing Services
30 Kimball Avenue
Suite 304
South Burlington, VT 05403
(802) 658-9111

TAD Technical Services
100 Dorset Street
Suite 14
South Burlington, VT 05403
(802) 658-5007

Williston
NorthStar Staffing Services, Inc.
P.O. Box 911
Williston, VT 05495-0911
(802) 879-6909

Triad Temporary Services, Inc.
P.O. Box 789
Williston, VT 05495
(802) 864-8255

VIRGIN ISLANDS

St. Croix
Alltemp Services, Inc.
Christiansted
Commerce Place 1
1142 King Street
St. Croix, VI 00820
(809) 773-9688
Fax: (809) 773-5361

VIRGINIA

Chesapeake
Aarow Temporary Services
3330 South Military Highway
Chesapeake, VA 23323-3500
(757) 487-8650
Fax: (757) 487-0604

Fairfax

Affinity Staffing, Inc.
3611-D Chain Bridge Road
Fairfax, VA 22030
(703) 691-1891
Fax: (703) 691-3282

Forest

Alpha Omega Resources
Route 221, Suite 14
Briarwood Business Center
Forest, VA 24451
(804) 385-8640
Fax: (804) 385-0192

Virginia Beach

A Plus Personnel, Inc.
Suite 201
5339 Virginia Beach Boulevard
Virginia Beach, VA 23462
(804) 456-5347
Fax: (804) 456-5570

Winchester

AES Corporate Services, Inc.
640 Airport Road
Winchester, VA 22602
(540) 667-2696
Fax: (540) 665-0768

WASHINGTON

Bellevue

Accounting Partners
Suite 1640
500 108th Avenue NE
Bellevue, WA 98004
(206) 450-1900
Fax: (206) 450-1056

Yakima

ADD Temporary Help Service, Inc.
408 West Chestnut
Yakima, WA 98902
(509) 452-6556
Fax: (509) 452-0231

WEST VIRGINIA

Charleston

United Talent, Inc.
428 Broad Street
Charleston, WV 25301
(304) 345-1515
Fax: (304) 342-4036

WISCONSIN

Green Bay

Allstaff, Inc.
Suite 7
2201 South Oneida Street
Green Bay, WI 54304
(414) 494-7823
Fax: (414) 499-4634

Madison

ABR Corporation
Suite 201
214 North Henry Street
Madison, WI 53703-2200
(608) 255-2436
Fax: (608) 255-0456

WYOMING

Casper

Olsten Staffing Services
800 Warren Court, Suite 170
Casper, WY 82601
(307) 237-3283

Cheyenne

Corestaff Services
2220 Dell Range Boulevard
Cheyenne, WY 82009
(307) 632-9155

Express Personnel Services
2205 East Pershing Boulevard
Cheyenne, WY 82001
(307) 634-1635

Fort Collins

Interim Services, Inc.
215 West Oak #103
Fort Collins, WY 80521
(307) 634-2899

Index